D1229683

12: PERSPECTIVES IN CRITICISM

PERSPECTIVES IN CRITICISM

1: *Elements of Critical Theory*

2: *The Disinherited of Art*

3: *Stream of Consciousness in the Modern Novel*

4: *The Poet in the Poem*

5: *Arthurian Triptych*

6: *The Brazilian Othello of Machado de Assis*

7: *The World of Jean Anouilh*

8: *A New Approach to Joyce*

9: *The Idea of Coleridge's Criticism*

10: *Introduction to the Psychoanalysis of Mallarmé*

11: *This Dark Estate: A Reading of Pope*

12: *The Confucian Odes of Ezra Pound*

12:

L. S. Dembo

The Confucian Odes of Ezra Pound

A CRITICAL APPRAISAL

UNIVERSITY OF CALIFORNIA PRESS
Berkeley and Los Angeles
1963

University of California Press
Berkeley and Los Angeles, California

LIBRARY OF CONGRESS CATALOG CARD NO. 63-12817
Printed in the United States of America
Designed by Ward Ritchie

For Tze-nan and I-ling

Acknowledgments

I AM particularly grateful for the encouragement and advice given to me by Professor John Espey ever since this study was conceived. I am also indebted to Miss Chia Fu-ming of the Teachers College, Taipei, Taiwan, who aided me in research and provided the calligraphy that appears throughout the volume, and to Mrs. Mok Yue Man-hing and Mr. Lin Che-hui of the Oriental Library at the University of California, Los Angeles, for coöperation far beyond that which I could rightfully expect. I wish to thank The Regents of the University of California for a faculty grant that gave me the time to complete the work. Finally, I am indebted to the Central Stenographic Bureau of UCLA for the efficient preparation of the manuscript for press, and to Miss Barbara Zeisl, who aided me in the proofreading.

Quotations from Pound's version of the Confucian Odes are from *The Classic Anthology Defined By Confucius* (Cambridge, 1954) and are published by permission of the Harvard University Press. Quotations from Arthur Waley's translations are all from *The Book of Songs* (New York, 1960) and are published by permission of the Grove Press and George Allen & Unwin Ltd.

Los Angeles, California L. S. D.
November 1962

Contents

1. *Introduction* 1

2. *The Confucian Poetic* 5

3. *Apocalyptic Translation* 20

4. *"Kuo Feng": Women* 36

5. *"Kuo Feng": Men* 63

6. *"Ya" and "Sung": State and Heaven* 80

Notes 107

1

Introduction

I AM not going to begin this essay by asserting that the subject has been unjustifiably neglected, its hidden merits overlooked, its significance underestimated. In a sense, the Confucian Odes have naturally resisted comment, both in quantity and quality, for generally the critic able to judge them as poetry is ill-equipped to judge them as translations, and the critic who can judge them as translations is rarely in a position to judge them on literary merit.[1] Furthermore, I am content to allow an essentially minor work to remain minor; but what I should like to do is to show that this work, perhaps more clearly than the *Cantos,* defines the achievement and the tragedy of Ezra Pound as a poet, an aesthetician, and an interpreter of the culture that he apotheosized. Pound's reasons for translating the three hundred and four odes of the *Classic Anthology* (to call the task arduous would be an understatement) constitute a poetic in themselves, a poetic closely related to a philosophy of history—in fact, of human experience in general—and correspondingly the methods that he used are derived from a particular theory of language worked out within this poetic. Pound's ability to put theory into practice, his ability to create what he constantly demanded must be created, is the subject of this book.

Ezra Pound's conception of the ideal translator was

no different from his conception of the ideal poet, who was supposedly charged with the almost divine mission of "rectifying" language and bringing about the psychological and social renovation that would mark a new "cultural synthesis" or "paideuma." Underlying most of Pound's remarks about the character and function of translation is this visionary notion of language—the idea of an apocalyptic mode of communication, associated with Order, Beauty, and Truth, in contradistinction to a common or unenlightened mode, associated with chaos, corruption, and illusion. The sense of Order, Beauty, and Truth (characterizing a paideuma) inherent in a specified original is apprehended only by a particular kind of translator and made manifest only by a particular kind of language. In effect, the poet-translator "intuits" a "state of mind" and recreates it in a "rectified" language; the common translator, adhering as he does to the syntax of the original, presents merely external information, the facts without the Truth, in a rhetorical and befogging idiom.

The justification for Pound's entire approach, as the justification for most of his theories, lies in the view that history is a chronicle of the achievement of an ideal Kultur (or paideuma) by the natural or good forces, and its corruption by the perverted or evil forces of the society. In regard to translation, the poet is inspired by direct empathy with the mind of the original author, in a sense his alter-ego, who voices the Kultur of his own epoch and therefore speaks to all epochs. As a method by which this cultural vision of one age is transmitted to another, translation becomes apocalyptic, a means of revealing the Reality behind the flux of history. In such revelation, achieved through the living idiom of the audience, lies the hope of society.

One can see how necessary to this kind of logic is hostility to the syntactically accurate translation. Pound devises the word "logopoeia" in describing *the* crucial problem of the translator. He asserts that he is referring to the use of words "not only for their direct meaning" but for "the context we expect to find with the word, its usual concomitants, of its known acceptances, and of ironical play."[2] He argues that this quality is untranslatable, but that if the state of mind of the native writer can be determined, an equivalent may be found. This argument is hardly new, but in theory and practice Pound has startlingly pursued its implications. The word "equivalent," seemingly innocuous, is in truth the foundation of his technique, and its ramifications become apparent when we find such renderings as "Don't chop that pear tree, / Don't spoil that shade; / Thaar's where ole Marse Shao used to sit, / Lord, how I wish he was judgin' yet."[3] There is more than whimsy in this kind of thing: the feelings of a Chinese peasant toward a benevolent lord are rendered by the equivalent of, ostensibly, an American Negro slave's feelings toward a benevolent master, in a language which Pound takes to be "living" dialect. It is more than a matter, here, of there being certain similarities between the two; the most scrupulous historian could concede the point without dishonor. But what has happened is that Pound has destroyed all sense of the differences. In seeking his "equivalent" he has in fact found perfect identity and has transcended all chronological barriers convinced that his rendering is an illumination reflecting the Truth of China and the Reality of history, even though to the Sinologue the reading is absurd. This example is somewhat extreme, I admit, but it at least shows what Pound is capable of doing, not out of ignorance, but guided by what amounts to a metaphysical bias.

In practice, the attempt to create an "equivalent" is ultimately reduced to the attempt to fashion a dramatic language, the effect depending, as Pound put it in regard to his translation of *The Analects,* upon "laconism and the sense of the live man speaking." One might go so far as to say that the preoccupation with form has here reached its limits, insofar as the very use of words has become an instrument of revelation. The "spirit" is captured, the mind illuminated, merely because the translator can write in an idiom vital to his audience. In reality, a live man speaking English may be no incarnation at all of an ancient Chinese, since the translator may be doing no more than substituting a set of foreign poetic responses for the native. That is to say, he may subvert an emotion that he either misunderstands or finds incomprehensible and replace it with one that would have been incomprehensible to the original author. In Pound's metaphysic, the distinctions become unimportant, since those emotions really necessary to moral and aesthetic life are taken to be the same in all ages, and the mission of the translator is completed when the reader is awakened to that truth.

When we come to look at the specific work that Pound has chosen to represent the Chinese paideuma, the *Shih Ching* or *Classic Anthology* supposedly edited by Confucius, we find ourselves confronted with another problem in point of view. For, in a sense, there are two *Shih Ching:* one defined by modern Western scholarship as a haphazard collection of songs, odes, and sacrificial pieces expressing the mores of Chou Dynasty China from the twelfth to the seventh centuries B.C.; the other defined by the Confucian school as a scrupulously edited work expressing a central moral vision of life. Schisms exist in the latter view, as they do in any ideology, but, for the most part, the *Shih* is characterized here as a document of scriptural importance. This is the view that has held almost total sway over the Chinese imagination for two and a half millenia; whatever the realities of the *Shih* as primitive poetry, it is its image that has really come to represent a paideuma, if anything does—and if we examine the context in which this image is set, we shall find, I think, the whole philosophic rationale behind Pound's encounter with the three-hundred-odd odes in the collection.[4]

2

The Confucian Poetic

It is true that Confucianism is a social philosophy, and commentators have been quick to indicate the analogue it presents to Pound's view of order in the state. Pound himself has spoken at length on the subject. But what his commentators have not indicated, or have indicated with all too little emphasis, is that it is a social philosophy with a profound psychological orientation. On the last page of Pound's translation, the reader will discover, in large characters, the imperative, "Think without evil" (*ssu wu hsieh*), a Confucian epigraph to the odes and, in essence, the first and last principle of the Confucian view of life.

That one may appreciate the subtleties behind this deceptively simple expression, I offer a characteristic trend of thought revealed in an exchange in *The Analects:*

> Tze-Hsia asked, "What is the meaning of the passage—'The pretty dimples of her artful smile! The lovely black and white of her eye! The plain ground for the colors?' "
>
> The Master said, "The business of laying on the colors follows (the preparation of) the plain ground."
>
> "Ceremonies then are a subsequent thing?" The Master said, "It is Shang who can bring out my

meaning. Now I can begin to talk about the odes with him." [1]

The dialogue opens with a question that could be asked only by a disciple of Kung (Confucius): it assumes that the lines necessarily have a meaning, esoteric and moral, beyond their literal statement. Kung's reply is only a slight rearrangement of the lines; a general principle seems to emerge, suggestive but elusive. It is Shang, the second disciple, who perceives at once all the implications of the reply: his question is the final step in an inductive leap from the particularized imagery of the poem to a moral truth in a crucial area of social relations. Just as the lines of the ode bring a revelation to Kung, so Kung's formulation of their truth brings a revelation to his disciple, one which elicits the highest praise the Master can bestow. Shang is now in a position to comprehend the "scripture" because his mind has achieved a discipline and insight approximating Kung's. The original Chinese, incidentally, is far less loquacious than the English translation. Kung replies to Tze-Hsia's question in only four words; Shang replies to Kung in only two (not counting the character that signifies interrogation). Such brevity creates a tension that is wholly in keeping with the revelatory nature of the exchange.

But let us look for a moment at exactly what is being said: "The business of laying on colors follows (the preparation of) the plain ground," or literally, "Silk matters follow plain." [2] Shang has identified the colors, or silk, with *Li* (ceremony), that ambiguous term suggesting the superstructure of ritualistic and conventional action that maintains social harmony, reflects order in the state, and puts man in unity with the processes of heaven. The plain ground to be prepared, the white surface upon which the colors must be painted, the root of which all social action is the branch, is the human mind or heart, as the famous passage in the *Adult Study* reveals:

> The ancients who wished to illustrate illustrious virtue throughout the kingdom, first ordered well their own states. Wishing to order well their states, they first regulated their families. Wishing to regulate their families, they first cultivated their persons. Wishing to cultivate their persons, they first rectified their hearts. Wishing to rectify their hearts, they first sought to be sincere in their thoughts. Wishing to be sincere in their thoughts, they first extended to the utmost their knowledge. Such extension of knowledge lay in the investigation of things.[3]

"The investigation of things" suggests an attempt of the mind to comprehend the basic principles inherent in things and therein apprehend the way of Nature. Once the mind apprehends Truth, it has the pattern to which it must adjust itself and can therefore seek to render its thoughts sincere and through sincerity to discipline its emotions. Upon this rectification, this cultivation of the mind so that it is in harmony with the way of the universe (the state of Virtue), moral action depends; without it, all responses and all conduct, whatever their appearance, are either hypocritical, overtly evil, or meaningless. The root always takes precedence over the branch, the emotion over the act. From this background emerges Shang's illumination.

In its suppositions about the odes, the dialogue in *The Analects* provides us with an entire theory of the function of poetry; in its content, with an entire theory of human nature. Both notions support each other. The implication here is, first, that the business of life is to rectify the mind, and second, that the primary aim of poetry is to exert a rectifying influence. Thus Kung's assertion: "In the Book of Poetry are three hundred pieces, but the design of them may be embraced in one sentence—'Think without evil' "; that is, with thoughts made sincere and the heart rectified, with the mind adjusted to the pattern of the universe and thereby in a state of Virtue. This, it seems to me, is the basis of the nine-word poetic, "stimulation by the odes; establishment by ceremony; maturation by music."

It is not surprising to find that in Confucian thought even a wholly aesthetic art, like music, becomes a psychological and moral force: "From a study of sounds, one comes to understand the tones; from a study of tones, one comes to understand music; and from a study of music, one comes to understand the principles of government and is thus fully prepared for being a ruler." [4] To appreciate that music and politics are intimately related, one must go back to the root of things. The study of sounds is part of man's investigation of nature, and the harmony of music and the harmony of the ordered polity are both manifestations of the Way. Ideal music is, in a sense, a music of the spheres that recreates in the mind the same harmony that pervades the universe. Accordingly, the harmonious mind must express itself in external acts by means of ceremony or ritual:

> To bring the people's inner feelings and their external conduct into balance is the work of rituals and music. The establishment of rituals gives a well-defined sense of order and discipline, while the general spread of music and song establishes the general atmosphere of peace in the people. . . .
>
> Rituals teach piety under different circumstances, and music teaches love in varying forms. When this moral condition is established through rituals and music, then we have a continuity of culture and the rise of different wise rulers.[5]

About this philosophic core there eventually crystallized an entire dogma, set forth in the prefaces to the so-called Mao edition, considered the standard version when the Anthology was reconstructed in Han times after the great book-burning of the preceding dynasty. Mythopoeic in extent, this dogma projected a total vision of history, politics, morality, and religion.

The Chinese view begins with the ambiguous term *feng* which means, literally, "wind," and, secondarily, "customs" or "manners" (*feng su*). Thus the first part of the *Shih,* called the "Kuo Feng," could be said to mean "customs of the states." In Confucian criticism, however, the distinction between "wind" and "custom" is eliminated, and done so in such a way that the title becomes the perfect expression of a process central to the philosophy. Here, for instance, is an explanation by Chu Cho, a fourteenth century commentator: "Feng means blowing. The wind blows men just as it blows objects and causes motion; thus the wind comes from one person and makes customs in a state." The "one person," as was mentioned earlier, is the Prince, upon whose sole influence depends the moral character of the state. In this sense, feng becomes the primary educative process: *kuo feng* is now understood not just as a description of manners but as a "lesson of manners." "Wind moves (things) and instruction transforms the people," says the Mao Preface.[6]

The behavior of the Prince creates a "wind" that establishes the character of the people, whose feelings are expressed in words that become poetry or song. The ideal Prince, behaving in accordance with the Will of Heaven (the *T'ien Ming*), establishes an ideal environment: harmonious emotions and proper customs are expressed in song, which, in turn, becomes an educative influence maintaining light in the society and bringing light to those dwelling under less fortunate rule. An ideal paideuma is achieved and the man, the state, and the universe are in harmony. When the Prince loses sight of the Way and ceases to act in accordance with the principles of the universe, an evil or "changed" wind (*pien feng*) blows, manners are corrupted, and poetry, either immoral or resentful, now serves as a warning that serious disharmony exists.

The psychopolitical bias of the Confucian argument is again apparent here. The Preface asserts:

Emotions spring from within and are embodied

> by words. When words are insufficient, they are expressed by sighs and exclamations; when sighs and exclamations are insufficient, they are expressed by extended song; when song is insufficient, hands move and feet dance unconsciously.[7]

I take this assertion to mean that, given the influence of the feng, the human heart will invariably express itself, the point being that the nature of the expression depends upon the kind of feng that is being exerted. Poetry, the inevitable response to a political condition, represents the psychological and moral state of the people and the general situation of the universe and, in addition, becomes a corrective. "To rectify gain and loss, to move Heaven and Earth, to arouse Spirits, nothing is nearer than poetry." Here is how the Preface accounts for the names of each of the four major divisions of the *Shih:*

"Kuo Feng" (Pound, "Folk Songs"):

> Superiors, by the Fung, transformed their inferiors, and inferiors, by them, satirized their superiors. The principal thing in them was their style, and reproof was cunningly insinuated . . . . hence they are called *Fung,* (or Lessons of Manners).

"Hsiao Ya" and "Ta Ya" (Pound, "Elegantiae" and "Greater Odes"):

> The pieces which speak of the matters of the kingdom, and represent the customs of its whole extent, are called the Ya. Ya means correct. They tell the causes why royal government decays or flourishes. In government there are great matters and small, and hence there are the small Ya and the great Ya.

"Sung" (Pound, "Temple Odes"):

> So called, because they praise the embodied forms of complete virtue, and announce to spiritual Beings its grand achievements. . . . These are called the four primary (divisions of the *Book of Poems*); (in them we have) the perfection of poetry.[8]

When the idea of feng was taken to be the central fact of history—specific history—the moral poetics of the *Shih* reached their most elaborate stage. This reading was based on the Confucian proposition that Chinese history entered a golden age with the founding of the Chou Dynasty by the archetype of the ideal ruler, Wen Wang, whose virtue was so great as to earn for him the Decree of Heaven (that is, the favorable expression of the T'ien Ming). Although it was actually his son, Wu, who carried out the war that ended in the overthrow of the Shang or Yin Dynasty, the achievement was attributable to the glory of the father. Wen's rule in the state of Chou, Wu's rule as king and his son Ch'eng's continuation of his policies after his death, a period spanning about a century, is considered to have been the great moral epoch, after which all else represented a gradual decline marked by weak central power and ambitious, warring feudatories. Since the kind of poetry written was a direct result of the feng of ruler in power, the odes supposedly written during the great age were considered "rectified" or "genuine" (*cheng*—as in *cheng ming*) [9] and those written in the period of decline, necessarily immoral or resentful, were considered "unrectified" or "changed" (*pien*). One can see, incidentally, how all the Confucian preoccupations come to a focus in the consideration of Chou history: the desire to restore central moral authority and the corresponding reaction against anarchy, in which vassals, by illegally attempting to usurp power, bring war to the society, corruption to the mind, and disorder to the universe. Kung saw his own epoch (the sixth century B.C.) as the culmination of social ruin in which the final collapse of the Chou Dynasty, reduced to a mere name, was imminent.

In the Confucian reading, the Anthology, as arranged by the Master, followed a pattern in keeping with the natural order of the universe. It began with the relationship of men and women and its culmination in the family; this was the "Kuo Feng," of which the first two sections, "Chou Nan" and "Shao Nan" were considered written during the time of Wen Wang and therefore cheng or genuine. The odes in twelve of the remaining sections were considered "postlapsarian" and therefore pien or changed; the final section, "Pin Feng," allegedly written by Chou Kung (Duke of Chou), another moral hero in the time of Ch'eng Wang, was considered indicative that salvation of the state was yet possible.

Following the folk songs are the "Hsiao Ya" (small ya), which represent the relations between the king and his ministers, both a prototype of and an influence upon the relations of the family, and the "Ta Ya" (great ya), which represent those between the king and heaven. As ceremonial odes and therefore an expression of customs, the ya, like the folk songs, are both genuine and changed; in the small ya, a changed ode would be an attack upon improper customs generated by the court; in the great ya, it would be an outcry against the disruption of natural order, say drought or famine, taken to be a direct result of the ruler's deviation from the proper rites by which universal harmony was maintained.

Finally, there are the "Sung" or temple odes, conceived as the direct communication with heaven by a virtuous society. Specifically, they are a "report" to ancestors and spirits of the times of peace and abundance following the establishment of the new dynasty. In a sense they represent a kind of inverse logos, in which the proof of apprehension of the Word, the Ming of Heaven, lies in its annunciation by the hearer and therefore becomes a rite in itself. The single moral theme binding all four books is that social salvation depends upon adherence to the rites established by Wen Wang, rites applicable to both family and state, divinely inspired and insuring divine harmony since they are the external reflection in human life of the Way of Nature. When a king adheres to such rites, he reveals that his mind is attuned to the Way and his feng becomes an irresistible, benevolent influence upon his subjects.

The Confucian logic has had to account for certain apparent exceptions to the idea that a changed ode must be either immoral or resentful since its writer lived in decadent times. A poem that appears in the Wei section, for instance, praises the virtues of the Prince (Ode 55) and another in the Cheng section (not to be confused with King Ch'eng) portrays the felicity of a married couple (Ode 82). Neither of these examples is isolated, and the latter is all the more significant for Kung's having singled out the songs of Cheng for explicit condemnation. The Confucian reply in both instances is characteristic: in regard to the Prince, he is indeed to be praised for his virtue, but one must still recognize that he is no more than the ideal servant of a degenerated emperor. His implicit weakness, one that is evidenced by the preponderance of obviously changed odes in the section, is that his feng, not being imperial, was insufficient to counteract that of the established ruler and to transform the whole society; that is, he is virtuous but not so virtuous as to be able to acquire the Decree of Heaven necessary for founding a dynasty and establishing a new moral and political order. In regard to the marriage ode, the Preface argues that it "sets forth the righteous ways of old times, to brand the character of the existing time which had no pleasure in virtue, and loved only sensual enjoyment." [10] Legge calls this view absurd, and perhaps it is, but it is the kind of absurdity that results from logical necessity: true marital harmony, a result of virtuous rule, cannot occur in a misruled state; therefore the ode is a product of a past age or else a vision of a past moral order—in short, a song of resentment, not felicity.

Implied in the Confucian response to both these odes is the tenet that poetic excellence and moral rectitude are intimately related. Truly good poetry cannot be produced in a decadent age, and, no matter what their content, changed odes can never equal the genuine in quality. Legge argues that "There are both in the Fung and the Ya many odes of a changed character, which by their spirit and style are equal to any of those that are ranked in the better class." [11] The observation may be accurate, but in another way is also quite naïve.

After asserting that the odes stimulate the mind, provide a means of self-contemplation, teach sociability, indicate how to regulate feelings of resentment, and serve as a model for filial piety and loyalty to the Prince, Confucius adds a final proposition: "From them we become largely acquainted with the names of birds, beasts, and plants." [12] This seemingly incongruous statement about the acquisition of physical knowledge in the midst of propositions concerned with moral education involves, of course, something more than the mere accumulation of facts; for it recalls the principle that the source of self-cultivation and social harmony lies in "the investigation of things." Herein appeared another facet of the revelatory poetics of the *Shih:* the myriad physical images, covering what was possibly the whole range of Chinese flora and fauna, each carefully named to preserve proper distinctions, represent a natural order corresponding to the psychological, familial, and political order ideally manifest in the human world. Proper names (cheng ming) maintain the distinctions between Prince and vassal, father and son, will and undisciplined emotion: all elements in the hierarchy of life are precisely named in order that relationships may be fully understood and the harmony of the Way apprehended by the "investigator." Knowing the names of birds, beasts, and plants thus has its importance.

In keeping with the assumption that natural images were signs as well as realities, Confucian criticism established three categories for denoting the ways in which these images might be used in the *Shih: fu,* the narrative style in which images had no meaning beyond their appearance; *pi,* the so-called "metaphorical" style in which images referred to something beyond themselves not stated in the poem; and *hsing,* the allusive style in which images appearing in an opening couplet and repeated in a refrain allude to or present an analogy to a subject explicitly discussed in the poem.[13] Although these terms provide only a very general framework for the Confucian approach, they are quite accurate as description, and I should like to consider some of their possibilities.

First, here is an example of an image treated in the allusive style (hsing), in which an analogy introduces the subject:

> The wind blows and is fierce.
> He looks at me and smiles,
> With scornful words and dissolute,—the smile
> of pride.
> To the centre of my heart, I am grieved.[14]
>
> (Ode 30, Legge)

The comparison is simple enough; the cold smile and scorn of the husband are like a fierce wind. Next, in Ode 35 (Legge), we find:

> Gently [or "gustily"] blows the east wind,
> With cloudy skies and with rain.
> (Husband and wife) should strive to be of the
> same mind,
> And not let angry feelings arise.[15]

Here the comparison, which affects our reading of the previous ode, seems to be between the wind and (1) the state of marriage, (2) the feelings of husband and wife (anger), and, again, (3) the husband himself, who is causing the strife. That is to say, an ambiguity exists in which all cases are included. In Ode 201, supposedly about one friend's abandoning another, there appears:

> Gently blows the east wind;—
> The wind followed by the rain.
> In the time of fear and dread,

It was all I and you.
In your time of rest and pleasure,
You have turned and cast me off.[16]

Line three introduces an interesting complication. The injured friend grieves because the other, who depended upon him in times of "fear and dread," has deserted him in times of "rest and pleasure." What happens, then, is that the storm simile represents not the past fear and dread, which actually were beneficial to the friendship, but the time of supposed ease, which has destroyed it. In any case, the ode supports the previous interpretation of the wind's referring to a social situation and to a state of mind.

Before drawing any conclusions, we might look at the treatment of the wind image in the "metaphorical" style (no referent stated for the image). Ode 41 begins:

Cold blows the north wind;
Thick falls the snow.
Ye who love and regard me,
Let us join hands and go together.
Is it a time for delay?
The urgency is extreme! [17]

This ode, says the Preface, "is directed against the cruel oppression which prevailed in Wei. . . . the common people could not keep together in their relative circles, but took one another's hands, and went away." [18] That is, they followed the common practice of fleeing a misruled state. In this sense, then, the wind refers to a political condition.

The image appears in several other odes in the same kind of context, and when all the possibilities are drawn together we find an evil wind representing a psychological state, situations involving friendship and marriage, and a political condition. Strictly speaking, these allegorical relationships ought to be as far as we go, but the reader has probably already surmised the next step, one that brings us out of the realm of allegory and into symbolism. Viewed in Confucian terms, all three winds coalesce into the single wind originating in the conduct of the Prince. In the first example (Ode 30), the scorn of the husband for his wife is but a manifestation on the family level of what is occurring on the political: when the lord of the state is corrupt, then so is the lord of the house; the failure of one to adhere to the proper customs leads to a similar failure in the other, signified by the husband's conduct toward his wife. Further, the behavior is merely an expression of confusion in the heart —the real source of chaos on each level of human experience—with excess pride in the Prince (husband) leading to despair and grief in the people (wife). When the feng of the Prince is evil, all human relations are in jeopardy—friends abandoned, wives mistreated, parents held in contempt.

It is this kind of interpretation, I think, that is really demanded by the Confucian poetic, even if the critical terminology brings us only part way. For it is the latent symbolism, or what the Chinese take to be latent, that has made the *Shih* the central cultural document that it is. The major premise, again, is that images are eventually, if not immediately, part of an organic whole, the signs by which Truth reveals itself. If we pursue that Truth far enough we will arrive at that conception on which the entire moral and metaphysical life of China is based, the duality of the Yin and Yang.

In the Chinese mythos, the Yin (Shadow) and the Yang (Light) are the originating forces of the entire creation, the dialectical Female (Yin) and Male (Yang) principles that are the source and model of harmony in all spheres of existence. Like Freudian images, images of Yin or Yang can be read into almost any physical object. For instance, the fish hawks (Ode 1) in their cry "Kuan, Kuan" (Pound, "Hid, Hid!") are taken as emblems of the marital felicity that will be attained when the Prince marries his ideal mate, or any lover marries his beloved. The cry reveals the sanction of the universe and intimates the recurrence on earth of the divine principle. Less obvious is the duality reflected in, say, a king's emissary (Yang) upon a black horse (Yin); the emissary, carrying out the will of the lord, urging on his horse, emblemizes a harmonious situation that partakes of the divine.

Any image that refers immediately to a moral virtue has its roots in the center of creation. Thus the passivity and reverence of a royal bride: "How great is that luxuriance, / Those flowers of the sparrow-plum! / Are they not expressive of reverence and harmony?"[19] Propriety in a royal bride, one recalls, is indicative of order in the state, and order in the state means that ideal marriage is possible. Other plant images carry a special moral, and eventually metaphysical, meaning; here are two that appear to be only descriptive or narrative:

> By the graceful sweep of these banks,
> With the southern hill, so calm in the distance,
> (Has the palace arisen), firm as the roots of a clump of bamboos,
> (With its roof) like the luxuriant head of a pine tree.[20]

The ode celebrates the completion of a palace, but the palace is merely a reflection of the lord: the bamboo traditionally symbolizes his purity and the pine his strength, both obviously Yang images. I do not think it would be beyond the Confucian critic to see in the calm southern hill a Yin image that could allegorically be made to represent the people. (Authority, feng, flows from the north to the south, as the comment on the Chou and Shao Nan tells us.) I do not want to tire the reader with the long list of animals, birds, trees, and constellations that have a special relevance, both moral and cosmological, in Chinese thought; the important ones will come up again during the discussion of the individual poems. At this point it is sufficient to appreciate how images in the *Shih* work in general—or how the Confucian scholar thought they worked.

The approach to imagery reveals the characteristic Confucian habit of viewing a literary work as nothing more than the sum of its moral components. This is not just a case of assuming that there is such a thing as allegorical poetry or poetry with a moral purpose: the assumption is that the allegory *is* the poetry. The first proposition of the Preface is that poetry is a product of the Will (*chih*), the mind directed to the pursuit of virtue. Sincere moral expression, in which the devices of fu, pi, and hsing are employed in a conventionalized metric, is virtually by nature poetry, since it represents a mind in harmony, or at least seeking harmony, with Nature. The accurately delineated image, perceived in its allegorical relevance, becomes the basis of the ideal poem in the good society, and the enlightened but "changed" poem of resentment in the bad. Its aesthetic effect is heightened, or perhaps even created, by an appropriate music, which, in turn, shares its moral characteristics.

3

Apocalyptic Translation

THE CONFUCIAN view was both an influence upon and an approximate analogue to Pound's own conception of poetry and experience. The aim of *The Cantos* is revelatory, and in the same general manner and the same general terms as Confucians traditionally perceived the aim of the Odes. The purpose of all poetry was the moral renovation of the mind, the radical condition from which the branches of an ordered state and an integrated Kultur would emerge. Once the mind perceived the Pattern it would act with virtue, but to see the pattern to begin with, it had to be purged of the corrosive ideas instilled in it by the forces of evil, the befogging "usurers" who destroyed true culture and corrupted language. The impulse of the Confucian mind to view all art, aesthetic or discursive, as an implement of education is reflected in Pound, and we find him making such assertions as:

> The function of music is to present an example of order, or a less muddied congeries and proportion than we have yet about us in daily life. Hence the emphasis in Pythagorus and Confucius.
>
> The magic of music is in its effect on volition. A sudden clearing of the mind of rubbish and the reestablishment of a sense of proportion.[1]

Within this general vision, history becomes a moral apocalypse and the *Shih* its literary embodiment. "Kung the Anthologist" transmits the paideuma of early Chou China, the Age of Virtue, and "Pound the Translator" sees himself carrying on the insight of Kung. The Age of Virtue is made possible by the ideal ruler, the center of all moral life, whose influence is irresistible; correspondingly, the ruler is ideal because of his vast capacity for attuning his mind to the Truth of the universe. There is no mention in Pound's prose of the term "feng," but his notion of the "*directio voluntatis*" is clearly analogous. As used in *Jefferson and/or Mussolini*, for instance, Dante's expression seems to mean the ability of the head of state to generate ideas that are convertible into action:

> The ideas of genius, or of "men of intelligence" are organic and germinal, the "seed" of scriptures.
>
> You put one of these ideas somewhere, i.e., somewhere in a definite space and time, and something begins to happen.[2]

Rule by "genius" involves a total dedication to the welfare of the people (the sense of responsibility characteristic of the rectified mind) and the ability to exercise authority effortlessly. This latter requires "right opportunism," the ability to comprehend and take advantage of realities without corrupting oneself. Thus Pound says of Jefferson: "No man in history had ever done more and done it with less violence or with less needless expenditure of energy." For, "He governed with a limited suffrage, and by means of conversation with his more intelligent friends. Or rather he guided a limited electorate by what he wrote and said more or less privately. He canalized American thought by means of his verbal manifestations."[3] This image of Jefferson bears no little resemblance to that of the ideal Confucian Prince who surrounds himself with sound advisors and rules effortlessly by rectified language (cheng ming) and by the natural influence of his own virtue. My point here is simply that in this view, what, in very broad terms, constitutes a paideuma for Kung's age also constitutes one for Pound's: a revived *Shih* becomes the instrument for revealing the ultimate identity of all true leaders in all epochs. Kung educates Chou China to the reality of Wen Wang; Pound "educates" his own age to the "reality" of Jefferson and Mussolini. Wen becomes the prototype of the latter two, just as Kung becomes the prototype of Pound himself.

Regarded from another aspect, the odes represented the essence of Chinese civilization, and indeed of all true civilization, because in their immediate reflection of the actual details of life they were the antithesis of "abstractionism," the central beclouding force in history. Kung, asserts Pound, "collected *The Odes* to keep his followers from abstract discussion. That is, *The Odes* give particular instances. They do not lead to exaggerations of dogma." [4] Their effect on the mind was "totalitarian" in the sense that they provided a total vision of the interrelations of idea and action, thought and fact, morality and actual social behavior—an organic view—and did so in poetry, the special language of reality:

> And herein is clue to Confucius' reiterated commendation of such of his students as studied the Odes.
>
> He demanded or commended a type of perception, a kind of transmission of knowledge obtainable only from such concrete manifestation.

And finally:

> The reason for reading the *Book of the Odes* . . . is that poetry is totalitarian in any confrontation with prose. There is MORE in and on two pages of poetry than in or on ten pages of any prose. . . . [5]

The reader of the odes will be faced with a vast number of poems dealing specifically with the details of peasant life, and for Pound, as perhaps for Kung, it is precisely in these details that a moral vision lies, and precisely in the quantity and repetition that effective education is possible. Only a particular kind of poetic mind could set itself to the task of rendering the entire collection and perhaps envisioning a kind of form in its apparent formlessness. When regarded as a totality, with its recurrence of themes, its seeming chaos of episodes and statements under which lies an unravelling pattern of revelation, its periodic celebration of the culture hero and condemnation of the historical villain based on special moral insight, its cyclical view of historical process, it is apparent that the Anthology could not but appeal deeply to the author of *The Cantos.* In essence, what Pound discovered in Confucian philosophy was an idea of order in which the mind, the state, and the universe were organically related, and, in the *Shih Ching,* a demonstration of that idea in action. It was this total conception of Kultur that was the universal in the Chinese paideuma. Just as the original was thought to have had a renovating effect on its audience then, so the translation that succeeded in reviving it—that is, succeeded because the translator comprehended the true significance of the language in which it was written and could find an English equivalent for it—so such a translation could not but have a similar renovating effect on a modern audience. In a sense, the odes are nothing less than an attempt to realize the thesis of *The Cantos,* actually to lay before the Western world proof that time and history have but one illumination for all men in all ages.

To Ernest Fenollosa, whose ideas are largely responsible for Pound's "ideogrammic" translation of *The Classic Anthology,* the Chinese language, by its very nature, embodied the quintessence of poetry. Or to use Pound's terms, the Chinese character was the perfect literary expression of the idea in action. As Fenollosa put it, the ideograph, as a pictorial representation of an idea, wedded "thing" to "action" or "provided vivid shorthand pictures of actions and processes in nature." The reader had before him, in a Chinese sentence, a moving picture of events in natural, dramatic succession; Chinese thus combined concreteness with the sense of "natural process," two qualities Fenollosa took to be essential to all poetry, which could be judged on the basis of how well it succeeded in bringing the reader back to the "fundamental reality of *time*":

> The more concretely and vividly we express the interactions of things, the better the poetry. We need in poetry thousands of active words, each doing its utmost to show forth the motive and vital forces. We cannot exhibit the wealth of nature by mere summation, by the piling of sentences. Poetic thought works by suggestion, crowding maximum meaning into the single phrase pregnant, charged and luminous from within.[6]

A great deal has already been written about Fenollosa's etymological interpretation of the ideograph, the end product of his poetic, and I wish to do no more than recall some of its characteristics as a preparation for certain conclusions. In this approach all Chinese characters are taken to be "shorthand pictures of actions or processes." "For example," writes Fenollosa, "the ideograph meaning 'to speak' is a mouth with two words and a flame coming out of it 言. . . . The sun underlying the bursting forth of plants = spring 春. The sun tangled in the branches of the tree sign = east 東. 'Rice-field' plus 'struggle' = male 男." [7] In reality, this is not merely descriptive analysis; it is description to prove an aesthetic and philosophic point: that the Chinese reader is put into immediate "touch" with the operations of nature as soon as he beholds the ideograph.

One of the difficulties with this poetic is that the etymology of a large number of characters is conjectural and therefore the reader may not have any idea of what he is beholding; another is that Chinese reading habits have much in common with reading habits elsewhere, and the "picture" of a commonly used ideograph no longer strikes the viewer as anything but the abstraction it represents. But most ironically, thousands of characters are constructed with phonological, not pictorial, elements.[8] The ideograph still represents a meaning, not a sound, but it takes the form it does only because its pronunciation approximates that of another character. One of Fenollosa's examples of the pictograph is horse, 馬 , pronounced "ma" in Mandarin, but there exists a whole series of characters containing this form, not because they have anything to do with horses, but because they are all pronounced "ma": 媽 (mother), 嗎 (interrogative particle), 罵 (to curse), and so forth.[9]

But whatever the inaccuracies of Fenollosa's theory, there is no denying that the character has always had, in the Chinese mind, a mysterious, charismatic quality, since its harmoniously arranged components had their origins in natural objects. One can easily see how the Chinese would have every inclination to view the ideogram as a pictorial manifestation of the pattern of the universe and to elevate calligraphy to the foremost position among the arts.

In any case, Pound tried to recreate in English the two poetic qualities that Fenollosa said inhered in Chinese: the concrete image and the sense of dramatic succession. He believed that here lay the essence of the communication of reality—the laconic immediate idiom that was the antithesis of abstract statement—and these qualities are the basis of the ideogrammic method as applied to the translation of the odes. In practice, two styles emerged: the lyrical, associated with the sense of the mysterious and divine, the Eleusinian or charismatic element in which the Chinese paideuma culminates; and the colloquial or dialectal, usually associated with the sense of injustice, although occasionally used to express other kinds of unelevated emotion. We might look first at an example of the former, an ode in which a lover whose lady has not kept a rendezvous addresses a love token she has given him (Ode 42). Here is the original, with the ideographs and literal translation included so the reader may appreciate some of the pertinent characteristics modified by Pound:

靜 Ching 女 nu 其 ch'i 姝 ch'u
Quiet girl how charming
俟 Ssu 我 wo 於 yu 城 ch'eng 隅 yu
Dated me at wall's corner
愛 Ai 而 erh 不 pu 見 chien
Love but not seen
搔 Tsao 首 shou 踟 ch'ih 躕 ch'u
Scratch head walk to and fro

靜 Ch'ing 女 nu 其 ch'i 孌 luan
Quiet girl how fair
貽 I 我 wo 彤 t'ung 管 kuan
Gave me red pipe
彤 T'ung 管 kuan 有 yu 煒 wei
Red pipe has sheen
說 Yueh 懌 i 女 nu 美 mei
Delights (and) rejoices (in) girl's beauty

自 Tzu 牧 mu 歸 kuei 荑 t'i
From pasture brought-back young-shoots
洵 Hsun 美 mei 且 ch'ieh 異 i
Truly beautiful and rare
匪 Fei 女 ju 之 chih 為 wei 美 mei
Not you . . r being beautiful
美 Mei 人 jen 之 chih 貽 i
(But) Beautiful person . . 's gift [10]

The stylistic principles on which this ode is constructed are fairly apparent: each line contains four characters (with occasional exceptions); each stanza contains four lines; an explicit parallel exists between the first lines of stanzas one and two, with only the final ideographs differing; the rhyme scheme is, for the most part, regular, even in the modern pronunciation. As to content, the ode seems to be nothing more than the song of a disappointed lover who does not express any particularly profound emotion. I might add, incidentally, that as recently as 1930 the reading of this poem was the subject of voluminous discussion by Chinese commentators. Here is Pound's rendering:

> Lady of azure thought, supple and tall,
> I wait by nook, by angle in the wall,
> Love and see naught; shift foot and scratch
> my poll.
>
> Lady of silken word, in clarity
> gavest a reed whereon red flower flamed less
> than thy delightfulness.
>
> In mead she plucked the molu grass,
> fair as streamlet did she pass.
>
> "Reed, art to prize in thy beauty,
> but more that frail, who gave
> thee me."

First, Pound has tried to render the so-called motion picture quality of the Chinese, mentioned by Fenollosa, by dividing each line into two idea or image complexes so that each side of the line would resemble, as far as possible in English, an ideogram, and the whole poem appear to be a flow of such ideograms. Thus, in the first line, "Lady of azure thought" seems to be one ideogram; "supple and tall," the other. In the second line the two ideograms might be "I wait by nook" and "by angle in the wall." The third line balances "love and see naught" with the parallel "shift foot and scratch my poll." Lines four and five speak for themselves; six may be said to balance an ideogram with a cesura; and nine sets off the subject of the sentence, "Reed," from the predicate, "art to prize in thy beauty," while ten is divided between an adverbial clause, "but more that frail," and its demonstrative qualifier, "who gave thee me."

Just as Fenollosa noted the "wealth of transitive verbs" that contributed to the dramatic quality of the Chinese, so Pound relies on active English verbs used with as much economy of expression as possible. Arthur Waley, for example, will write, "But she hides and will not show herself"; Pound, "Love and see naught." And whereas Waley will say, "She has been in pastures and brought for me rush-wool," Pound will strip the line to "In mead she plucked the molu grass." [11] Accordingly, Pound uses the technique of direct quotation in laconic language in the present example as well as throughout the odes. Even the last two lines of Ode 42 are prolix in comparison to these from Ode 95:

> "The play?" says she.
> "Seen it." says he.
> "If so, let's go
> Over Wei
> pleasantly."

Or, from Ode 82:

> "Cock crow!" she says.
> He says: " 'Tis dark."
> "Up, sir," she says,
> "Up, see [sir?], get out
> and shoot the geese that be flyin' about."

But perhaps most important of all, the reader may have been taken by the lyrical quality of Pound's images, a quality that seems to transcend its original inspiration. What has happened is that refusing to render the abstraction for which the character stands, even denying that such an abstraction could have existed in the mind of the original reader, Pound has translated the pictorial elements of the character—or rather has rendered them etymologically, pseudoetymologically, one had better add. The abstraction "quiet lady," presented by the two ideographs 靜 女 with which the poem opens, has been rendered "Lady of azure thought." Azure comes from the left side of the ideograph 青 (ch'ing), a word in itself. Pound has assumed that "azure" and tranquillity are somehow identified, but, strictly speaking, ch'ing is a phonetic, not a pictograph. "Lady of silken word" is Pound's rendering for 孌

(luan) meaning "lovely." The bottom part of the character 女 is indeed the word for lady; the left and right middle 糸 is the root affixed to all words referring to silk, and 言 that affixed to all words associated with speaking—so that with the exception of the top 亠 (meaning roof), the character, pictorially, can be made to come out as Pound says it does, although the sense that he has given it is clearly not that intended in the original.

The truth is, of course, that this kind of lyricizing cannot be called a stylistic device and nothing more, for it has a profound effect on the total meaning of the ode. A modest maid may be a modest maid, but a Lady of Azure Thought is something else again. "Azure" has particular connotations for Pound, associated as it is with the light imagery that plays a large part, as one critic has observed, in *The Cantos*.[12] The total effect in the translation is that the girl ceases to be a reticent country maid, as the original would suggest, and emerges virtually as a mysterious goddess of light in the eyes of the beholder: "gavest a reed whereon red flower flamed less / than thy delightfulness." It doesn't matter that "flamed less" is another etymological translation; the total effect remains the same. Similarly, in her brightness, the maid is associated with the very components of nature, the sky, a flower, a "streamlet"—and takes on their pristine, elemental quality. She plucks not "young shoots," as in the original, but "molu grass" (or moly), a mythical herb with magic powers.

If Ode 42 is in fact no more than a folk song, then Pound's reading, for all its charm, considerably distorts the original. To the Confucian mind, however, a folk song selected for the Anthology by the Master always has a meaning deeper than the apparent one, and in the orthodox interpretation the point of the ode is taken to be its praise of the girl for resisting the temptation to meet her lover. In her virtue, she is supposedly a fit mate for a prince. What has happened is that this apparently trivial and isolated rural incident actually has become an index to the entire moral condition of the society, and the girl a symbol of its hope.[13] Since virtue in the people reflects virtue in the Prince and virtue in the Prince reflects harmony with the Way, a single profound moral force binding man to heaven, the attitude of the girl, which expresses this force, becomes almost charismatic. She is not a maid, but the very embodiment of a mystical and divine purity. If Pound has done nothing else in his lyricizing of the original he has indeed recaptured a Western equivalent for the kind of emotion that would be associated with the ultimate meaning of the Chinese moral experience. And it seems to me that here in the lyrical mode – pseudo etymology notwithstanding – lies his greatest strength as a poet and translator.

Pound hardly accepted the Confucian idea that an ode was nothing more than the sum of its moral components, and the crucial literary problem for him was to transform allegorical relationships into aesthetic entities so that they became as evocative to a metaphysically uninvolved western audience as they were, in the original, to an involved Chinese audience. Here is how the wind image, discussed in the last chapter, comes out in the lyrical style:

> Cold parcheth the end wind, colder mockery,
> Frigid the smile to my heart's misery. . . .
> The wind has blown the sky
> to one black solid cloud, all the day long
> night long I sleep not
> seeking to mutter this wrong. (Ode 30)

"End wind" is Pound's translation for *chung feng*, believed to mean a wind that blows all day. *Chung* itself does mean "end," but there is really no such thing as an end wind in either Chinese or English. The original implication may very well have been a wind that blows until the end of day—and Pound will, as a point of doctrine, seek out what he thinks is the etymological basis.

One is reminded here of his assertion that English literature lives on translation: "end wind" is a new word, supposedly evoking an ancient Chinese insight, and designed to have an impact upon the reader even though he does not entirely appreciate its reference.

Pound similarly makes explicit what does not exist or what is at best only implied in the original. The idea of a wind being so cold that it burns ("parcheth") and that the mockery of the lord is even colder yet represents a modern use of imagery that is rarely found in the *Shih*. Pound has also drawn out the character *yi*, meaning simply "obscurity," to arrive at "The wind has blown the sky / to one black solid cloud," a lyrical recreation of a line that is actually a refrain in the song. The entire impulse of this kind of translation is to revive the sense of mystery in the relation of the internal and external worlds that the Chinese ostensibly felt on the mere projection of the allegory in music and ideogram. Hence the concluding stanza, which one would never suspect is part of a song:

> Under black solid cloud,
> thunder, thunder so loud I sleep not,
> seeking to speak its thought.

This technique is apparent in Pound's handling of wind imagery in the other examples cited above. Odes 35 and 201 have identical opening lines, a common phenomenon in a poetry relying heavily on conventions and traditional formulae. The original is "Gently blows the east wind"; for the rendering in Ode 35, concerned with the lament of a peasant woman, we find: "Wind o' the East dark with rain, / a man should not bring his olde wife pain / but should bide concordantly." But in Ode 201 the same line is rendered, "Soft wind of the vale / that brings the turning rain, peril, foreboding." What is important in the peasant woman's speech, as fashioned by Pound, is not just the allegorical relationship as such, but the aura set forth; both introductory image and literal development do more than blankly present a formula; they actually recreate the feeling associated with formulary utterances. The woman invokes direct, simple truth out of folk wisdom, a truth that, expressed as it is, has the moral universe behind it. In the second example, Pound uses an adjective of his own that again pushes the image beyond the reaches of simple allegory: "Soft wind of the vale" is not formulary but descriptive. And because Pound is concerned primarily with descriptive impact, the same line is, for the sake of variety, transformed in succeeding stanzas into "Idle the valley wind" and "Scorching breath on the height." To recapitulate: the strength of Pound's version lies in imagery that charges the original allegorical relationships with an emotional quality perceptible to a Western audience, the intent being to give an insight into the final meaning of the Chinese experience whether or not the reader is aware of the details of the Confucian view.

On the other hand, an entirely different mode of writing appears throughout the translation as Pound's response to a particular kind of ode in the *Shih* and, it would seem, in response to a particular need within himself. Here is the climactic sixth stanza from Ode 200, a typical attack upon slanderers:

chuck 'em
to wolves and tigers, and if the striped cats
spew 'em forth,
Offer 'em to the Furthest North.
If the old pole decline to spare 'em place,
kick 'em clean off it into stellar space.

The poem concludes, conspicuously, "Meng Tsy has lost his balls but makes this verse, / let the administration heed it, or hear worse." It is not difficult, I think, to see the reasoning behind this kind of rendering. In a sense, the speaker, victimized by slanderers and dealt a customary punishment—the honest man victimized in a corrupt state where language has lost all meaning—is a persona of the poet in the world seen by Pound.

Rendered impotent, alone at "Willow Hollow Road by Acre Hill," with the one clear voice in a society that listens only to slanderers and exists only on corrupt language, he makes his verse.[14] In other words, the situation was particularly meaningful to Pound and it had to be made particularly meaningful to his audience; an idiom was necessary that would directly involve the reader with the material and so function as a mode of revelation. One had to feel the magic qualities of Virtue; one had to share the indignation of the Honest Man; only in such a way could the Chinese vision be revived.

Although a lyrical and colloquial ode might have the same poetic behind them, they are not necessarily of equal quality. The problem here is not that of superior and inferior genres, but of genuine and spurious diction. Here is an excerpt that reveals all too clearly the ends to which Pound will go in the belief that he is writing in a dramatic and realistic idiom:

> Pitch out the slimers and scare off worse,
>
> . . . .
>
> Throw out the punks who falsify your news,
> scare off the block-heads, thugs, thieves and
> screws.
> Don't shove it off on the working man,
>
> . . . .
>
> and don't promote the snots to sin on sly.
>
> (Ode 253)

Is this the voice of "The Duke of Mu to his colleagues in the ministry" or of Ezra Pound broadcasting? A version like this one violates more than just the syntax and imagery of the original; unlike the lyric, it is wholly out of harmony with the tone of anything written in the *Shih,* a tone that reflects the Chinese demand to maintain the dignity of the speaker however condemnatory his words. Even here one might forgive Pound if he had succeeded in creating an independent poem, but by reducing the language to the baldest and tritest kind of vituperation he leaves the reader with nothing. Nor do I think one can justify this reading on the basis that Pound is actually trying to fashion a persona, for if he is it is a very ineffective performance indeed.

Were these odes merely isolated examples, the whole problem could be dispensed with in a footnote, but "colloquial" diction plays a large role in Pound's translation. Furthermore, it occasionally appears in poems that are otherwise wholly lyrical, as it does in the concluding line of Ode 42 ("but more that frail who gave thee me"). My point is not that a genuine colloquial diction has no place in the Anthology; quite the contrary. I am simply questioning Pound's ability to put theory into practice. There is no little irony, I might add, in the fact that the greatest advocate in modern poetry of "rectified language" would have us accept banalities as a mode of revelation.

In the following chapters I should like to look more closely at Pound's success and failure as a translator of Chinese and as a poet. The focus of interest is upon the rhetorical methods used to render some of the major genres that appear in the Anthology, and the different effects achieved among poems within a genre. We turn first in the "Kuo Feng" to the love or courtship odes; then to the bridal poems or epithalamia; and finally to the marriage poems, which include the songs of separation and the desertion laments or wife's complaints. In the succeeding chapter we look at those genres dealing with men alone: the soldier's lament, the disaffected official's lament, and the various panegyrics and odes of censure. The study concludes with a chapter on the ya and sung, which, since they represent extensions of the techniques discussed in the "Kuo Feng" and partly overlap in theme, are treated in less detail. In establishing the categories of the love odes, I have followed the Confucian view, but one should keep in mind that the Chinese is often so ambiguous as to preclude our knowing whether the action involves boy and girl or man and wife. When the occasion requires, particularly when the tone of the translation suggests a nontraditional view, I have also given the alternate reading.

I should warn the reader that the approach I have taken requires an inordinate amount of quotation and an often tedious dwelling on detail. Although I cannot guarantee that his patience will be satisfactorily rewarded, I hope he will gain enough to read through this strange metamorphosis of a central cultural document without being intimidated by its obscurities.

4

"Kuo Feng": Women

COMMENTING ON the love odes, Marcel Granet writes:

> Not a single picture suggests a particular individual. A pronoun, the word "lord," ready-made phrases such as a handsome fellow, the pure maiden, the modest girl . . . the fair lady, serve in almost every instance to indicate the loved one. . . .
>
> These impersonal lovers express only impersonal sentiments . . . *sentimental themes*, such, for instance, as meetings, betrothals, quarrels and separations. These events are common to all, and all, men and women, react to them in the same way. No heart feels any individual emotion, no case is peculiar, no one loves or suffers in a fashion all his own. All individuality is absent and there is no attempt at any individuality of expression.[1]

This phenomenon, natural to a folk idiom, was fully conducive to the kind of interpretation made by the orthodox scholars who saw in the songs, when originally produced, an expression of the moral state of the people and, when anthologized, a means for regulating the behavior of men and women. Aside from the musical accompaniment, the chief interest was in the situation presented, the common event about which judgments could be made almost mechanically. As a Western poet, however, Pound was wholly inclined in the opposite direction: in creating not standardized figures who are without identity, but personae who, by revealing individual emotion, themselves become the center of interest. I do not mean that personal and immediate emotion read into a situation by Pound cannot finally be interpreted in a general manner; on the contrary, only by referring to the Chinese can we discover the full significance of an ode. But even in those genres, like the panegyric, that are wholly public in character, a poeticizing process is at work.

In the brief song called "Moonrise" (Ode 143), a balladeer declares his longing for a maid, whose splendor he compares to the moon, and is duly condemned by the Preface for his licentiousness. The three quatrains are repetitious, depending as they do upon parallelism, and nothing more is established than the fact of longing and the moonlike quality of the girl. Pound gives us this reading:

> The erudite moon is up, less fair than she
> who hath tied silk cords about
>   a heart in agony. . . .
>
> My heart is tinder, and steel plucks at my pain
> so all my work is vain,
>   she at such ease
>   as is the enquiring moon.

An etymological analysis will show how Pound got his images. From the character 皎 "bright" he has come up with "erudite" (白 "clear" or "white"; 交 perhaps taken as 狡 "clever"). He has taken the top part of 勞 "toil" as 火 "fire" to give us "tinder"; and it would seem he has broken 懰 "melancholy" into 金 "metal," 忄 "heart," and 刂 "knife" for the line "steel plucks at my pain." But quasi etymology or not, only a poet familiar with the Renaissance love lyric, or, more recently, with the poetry of Jules Laforgue, could call the moon "erudite" or change "The moon comes forth and shines; / How brilliant is that beautiful lady" (Legge) to "A glittering moon comes out / less bright than she the moon's colleague." The translation is not a folk song but a canzone, and the reader's attention is directed not so much to the "licentious" situation or even to the lady, but to the feelings of the speaker.

Whether Pound wants us to evaluate the situation as well as appreciate his technique, I cannot say, but there is room here for moral interpretation insofar as the profane lover is in perpetual torment and the ultimate Confucian value, perceived and celebrated by Pound, is serenity. Considered in terms of the Chinese paideuma, the romantic lover, far from being ennobled by his passion, is damned. Thus Kung said in *The Analects* that he had never seen one who loved virtue more than he loved beauty, and in fact the translation introduces the idea that to pursue beauty alone is to pursue the personification of impermanence, "of transient grace, / at ease, undurable, so all my work is vain / torn with this pain." Read in this light, the translation, presenting dramatically an image of the "unrectified" mind, goes even deeper than the original in its Confucian implications. Only madmen fall in love with the moon.

If "Moonrise" is indeed a vision of profane love, its perfect counterpart, a vision of idealized, sacred courtship, is presented in Ode 1, perhaps the most celebrated song in the Kuo Feng and able to be recited at a moment's notice by virtually any educated Chinese. Here is a possible literal rendering:

> "Kuan, kuan," cry fish hawks,
> In river's isle
> Shy and lovely girl
> Lord's good mate.
> Uneven grows hsing plant
> Left, right seek it,
> Shy and lovely girl
> Waking, sleeping seek her,

Seek her, not obtain,
Waking, sleeping think of her . . .

And Pound's equivalent:

"Hid! Hid!" the fish-hawk saith,
by isle is Ho the fish-hawk saith:
"Dark and clear,
Dark and clear
So shall be the prince's fere."

Clear as the stream her modesty;
As neath dark boughs her secrecy,
reed against reed
tall on slight
as the stream moves left and right,
dark and clear,
dark and clear.
To seek and not find
as a dream in his mind. . . .

As in Pound's version of Ode 42, discussed in the preceding chapter, the lady emerges here as a vision: she is "dark and clear" (an innovation based upon nothing in the text), mysterious, elusive, ghostly, and elemental in her purity—associated with the world of nature and with the Yin and Yang. Allegorically, the fish hawks stand for conjugality; "kuan, kuan," says Legge, are thought to be the harmonious notes of the male and female answering each other, and in Pound's treatment they acquire an oracular aura. What has happened, then, is that Pound has used a balladesque idiom, with chanting, repetitive rhythms and an appropriately evocative diction, to create the image of a folk charisma, to give the illusion of an unself-conscious, semimystical balladry. But even though it presents a contrast to the idiom of the egocentric love lyric, self-conscious or "literary" balladry, as readers of, say, Coleridge's "Ancient Mariner" will testify, almost always diverts interest away from the "situation" and toward the psychological elements inherent in it. And that is exactly the plane on which Pound's rendering seeks its effect. One has the sense of the total action of the poem—the cry of the fish hawks, the vision of the secret lady, the anticipation of winning her—occurring within the imagination of the Prince, literally "a dream in his mind." The Western poet can come no closer to making personal the essentially impersonal nature of the original ballad, and neither has Pound violated Confucian reading here any more than he has in the rendering of "Moonrise." As psychologically oriented as it is, Ode 1 is no love poem in the usual sense. The balladesque idiom virtually insures our reading the "torment" of the Prince as something ritualistic and impersonal, attached not to a woman but to a social charismatic or sacred image, an aesthetic equivalent for an allegorical Virtue. The quest of the Prince is for an ideal mate and has nothing to do with romantic love; once the ruler begins to think about his potential wife as a woman, the society is in trouble.

When Pound is at his best, the accentuation of feeling that is the usual effect of his technique, rather than clashing with the Chinese meaning, gives a legitimate equivalent. Consider, for instance, this way of translating the song called "Falling Plums," in which a girl announces her availability, the marriage season having arrived:

"Oh soldier, or captain,
Seven plums on the high bough,
plum time now,
seven left here, 'Ripe,' I cry.
Plums, three plums,
On the bough, 'Plum time!' I cry.

'No plums now,' I cry, I die." [2] (Ode 20)

This is no mere announcement of one's availability for marriage; it is a cry of desperation in which the girl has identified herself, her life, with plums on the tree, and is somehow caught up in the order of nature. The pathos is personal, but it also suggests something beyond itself. Legge tells us that scholars believed the issue to be not just marriage, but marriage in the proper season, "in accordance with propriety." The desperation of the girl (as persona) makes a great deal of sense in light of this view, for the rites are the very medium in which the private, public, and divine worlds come together, and her inability to follow them has implications that transcend secular life. For the Chinese, the real center of interest is the moral situation, and, as a matter of fact, one commentator asserts that the lady is not speaking in her own person, but represents any marriageable girl; for Pound, the center of interest is the response of the character to the situation and his aim, as I have said, is to dramatize individual emotion. In other words, he has destroyed a folk song (which necessarily expresses collective or "situational" feeling) in order to create a sophisticated Western lyric, the latter, however, remaining dependent upon the Chinese background for its ultimate significance.

If any single theme underlies the courtship odes (and indeed all the odes) it is the imperative to adhere to the rites, but consistency of theme has not prevented Pound from employing an endless number of devices to express a variety of moods and feelings. By no means does accentuation of feeling always move in the direction of the mysterious or elevated, nor is it always so intense as in the love lyric; on the other hand, neither are some of Pound's equivalents as just as others, to say the least. Here is a girl refusing to complete the marriage arrangements because her suitor has not fully complied with the rites:

> The sparrow has no horn to bore a hole?
> Say you won't use your family pull!
> Not for the court and not for the bailiff,
> shall you make me a wife to pay with.

Toothless rat, nothing to gnaw with?
And a whole family to go to law with?
Take me to court, see what will come.
Never, never, never will you drag me home.[3]

(Ode 17)

One may well wonder why the speaker should want to drag her home in the first place—at least judging from the persona that has been created here. To the Chinese there is no question of the girl's nature, for in her insistence lies the moral strength of a nation, and the Preface has gone so far as to assert that the ode reveals the end of a period of moral decay. But in accentuating her anger, at the expense of her dignity, Pound has given us the image of a rather hysterical young woman. The Western reader may or may not share Pound's delight in such an image, but as an equivalent it is a tax on anyone's credulity.

As rendered by Pound, Ode 17 represents a type: a semi- or quasi-rustic picture in which one is expected to respond to the diction of the speaker and to the "situation"; the emotion is not elevated and one is to appreciate the "human" rather than the charismatic qualities portrayed. Here is Ode 9 in which another country maid spurns her suitor:

Tall trees there be in south countree
that give no shade to rest in
And by the Han there roam young maids
to whom there's no suggestin'

that they should wade the Han by craft
or sail to Kiang's fount on a raft.

Both rhythm and rhyme scheme preclude our taking the speaker very seriously. Even though he has "piled high the kindling wood / and cut down sandal trees / to get this girl to take a man," the maid's final reply is again, "One does not wade the Han by craft / or reach the Kiang-fount on a raft." But with all its charm and apparent levity of mood, the rendering is deceptive, for when we look at it closely we can scarcely make any sense of the refrain. Exactly what does the girl's reply signify beyond outright denial? The suggestion seems to be that for her to marry the speaker would be like crossing the Han by "craft" (can one "wade" by craft?) or sailing up the Kiang (literally "river") on a raft, a difficult feat, we might assume. In this sense, the image is a metaphor: the suitor is as inadequate as a raft on the Han. But as the speaker uttered the expression (quoted above) in the first place, the meaning was simply that by crossing the Han she would be going home with him, the image being literal. Here is Waley's version:

> Beyond the Han a lady walks;
> One cannot seek her.
> Oh, the Han it is so broad,
> One cannot swim it,
> And the Kiang, it is so rough
> One cannot boat it!

The obscurity disappears, and so, unfortunately, does the charm.[4]

In Pound's version, the speaker seems to be doing all he can, and the refrain, especially put in the mouth of the girl at the conclusion of the last stanza, dramatizes the stubbornness with which he is faced—an accentuation similar to that which occurred in the case of the angry bride-to-be. But far from carrying us beyond the Confucian orbit, the ode, despite its distortions, becomes meaningful only when we appreciate the orthodox view. The girls of the Han, once licentious, have been transformed by the feng of Wen Wang, whose influence has extended (as the title of the section, "Shao and the South," would imply) to the southernmost parts of the empire. Legge suggests that the maid is not to be won by menial tasks performed for her by the suitor and will not surrender until the proper rites are followed. With this notion in mind we can make sense of the refrain; the girl's yielding to the suitor because of the menial tasks would be no different from crossing the Han by craft; as other odes indicate, marriage without proper rites usually ends in disaster, just as, we might suppose, crossing the Han by craft will end in drowning. I am not trying here to complicate the simple; we must remind ourselves continually that we are dealing with a sophisticated English poetry, the achievement of which lies in the illusion of simplicity that it fosters.

The ability of the lady to give a correct answer or to make a proper refusal, signifying her knowledge of and adherence to the moral order, is a Confucian touchstone for virtue. "Men rather trust girls' wits / who know the rules" and the fate of the unknowing or licentious maid is desertion and loneliness. Odes expressing the pathos of the country girl present the more common, if darker side, of the courtship ritual (more common because only the two opening sections reflect the golden age of Wen). Pound follows Karlgren's meaning in this typical translation:

> Dry grass, in vale:
> "alas!
> "I met a man, I
> met
> a man.
> "Scorched, alas, ere it could grow."
> A lonely girl pours out her woe.
>
> "Even in water-meadow, dry."
> Flow her tears abundantly,
> Solitude's no remedy. (Ode 69)

The intricate rhythm and internal and false rhyming testify to Pound's inability to render a simple lyric as a simple lyric. The original is in the third person and Pound has resorted to a favorite dramatizing device, balancing direct quotation against narrative statement. A contrast between the scorched grass with which the girl compares herself and the flowing tears, presented as it is in a laconic, partly imagistic fashion, virtually creates a moment out of an abstraction.

But of all the *pastourelles*, the most well-known to the Chinese is "Dead Deer in the Wilderness," an ode that defines the whole problem of pathetic maidenhood, or would if we could resolve its ambiguity:

Lies a dead deer on younder plain
whom white grass covers,
A melancholy maid in spring
                                        is luck
                                        for
                                        lovers.

. . . .

                              dead as doe is maidenhood.

(Ode 23)

A dead deer may be wrapped in white grass by the peasants, but a maid is not "in white mat bound, / as a jewel flawless found" when she is ravished. As Waley puts it, "there are men who 'kill' a girl, in the sense that they seduce her and fail to 'cover up' the damage by marrying her." [5] The question is whether the girl is being described by a knowing speaker who foresees her doom, or whether she is the speaker herself and reveals a knowledge of what might happen if she is careless. If the former, her case would seem hopeless; if the latter, she may be saved by her self-knowledge. Because the ode is part of the "Shao and the South," and therefore considered "rectified," the Preface takes an approving view, but the way in which the conclusion is rendered in Pound's English will convince the reader of nothing:

Hark!
Unhand my girdle-knot,
stay, stay, stay
or the dog
          may
          bark.

The original is not so obvious as this rendering would lead one to believe, and the orthodox scholars are satisfied that the girl means what she says. There is even doubt as to whether the word here rendered as "girdle-knot" actually refers to anything on her person—a state of affairs that speaks for itself. In any case, Pound's version of this ode contains a pathos that the reader can take seriously, but here is another way he treats the same subject:

> Hep-Cat Chung, 'ware my town,
> don't break my willows down.
> The trees don't matter
> but father's tongue, mother's tongue
>   have a heart, Chung,
>   it's awful. (Ode 76)

This is one of the songs of Cheng, which, Pound tells us, "Kung-fu-tsy seems to have regarded . . . a species of crooning or boogie-woogie," and that, I assume, accounts for the "Hep-Cat" and the kind of rhythm and rhyme scheme in the last three lines. (Actually, "tongue" and "Chung" do not rhyme, since the latter is pronounced "joong.") Ostensibly the girl is speaking in a language appropriate to her "licentious" character, but the situation is here rendered in such a way as to evoke nothing but a smile. Unfortunately, I am not sure that one does not end up smiling only at the dated slang, which gives the ode, slight though it may be, a false ring.

Even on the level of bathos, Pound seems not really to be judging the maid, or, to make matters more complicated, the tone would suggest an eye-winking sympathy for her. But odes of this nature troubled the scholars no less than the modern reader and their argument always took the form that Confucius expected the audience to judge for itself.[6] I am not certain that Pound expected the same from his own audience, since his adverse judgments are generally expressed in an irony that is unmistakable, and as far as simple pastoral licentiousness is concerned, the worst we can expect from him is mild satire:

On comes her car with a rattle-de-bang,
woven leather like cinnabar,
Loose, loose, a flaming star,
id est, Miss Ts'i shooting the moon
to Lu. . . .

Miss Ts'i and Lu Road we see
both wider than all liberality. (Ode 105)

Whatever his commitment to Chinese philosophy, Pound was too much the romantic to look upon this behavior with indignation, and we find him slipping into a lyrical idiom even when he is supposed to be translating an ode that is part of a collection labelled by him "mildly satiric":

Sun's in the East,
her loveliness
Comes here
To undress.

Twixt door and screen
at moon-rise
I hear
Her departing sighs. (Ode 99)

Pound may well be expecting us to read implications into this ode, but I'm more inclined to think his real interest was in creating another aesthetic "moment." As it stands, the poem has nothing satirical about it, with the possible exception of the title, "Town Life." And this is not the only ostensibly licentious poem that depends solely on lyricizing for its effect; here is another ode with a casual, mildly satiric title, "Rendezvous Manqué," and another aesthetic moment that belies it:

Neath East Gate willows
'tis good to lie.
She said:
"this evening."
Dawn's in the sky.

Neath thick willow boughs
'twas for last night.
Thick the close shade there.
The dawn is axe-bright.
(Ode 140)

Pseudo etymology (晢 "bright" taken as "axe-bright" from its 斤 component) is a usual sign that Pound is trying to create a lyrical situation. The dawn with its axe-bright rays has cut down the thick willow forest of night and anticipated love. That Pound is fully capable of turning this very situation into an epiphany (as the Confucians themselves are) we have seen in the last chapter in his rendering of Ode 42 called, in fact, "Appointment Manqué."

Marcel Granet has asserted that the love song had its origin in annual courtship contests or "proverb competitions" in which each of the opponents tried to establish a "correspondence between the proposition he hopes to make the successful one and a series of hallowed sayings which cannot be gainsaid without a certain suspicion of irreverence." The proof of the love-proposition was made by "analogic rhythm" or what amounted to a magical utterance or formula that revealed the associations of the speaker's suit with the ultimate principles of nature:

> The correspondences inscribed in the poetical themes showed the unity of natural and social rules, and their authority came from this. Human observances were endowed with new majesty because their force seemed to penetrate into the domain of Nature. Natural events in their turn assumed a moral value and served as *emblems* for the rules of social life.[7]

Pound's sensitivity to the conception of the song as a magical utterance is nowhere more apparent than in his treatment of the betrothal odes, in which the quality of decorum is raised to a mystery. This is not quite the same thing as analogic rhythm, but the translation does seek to endow a human observance "with new majesty." Here is one mode of expression that in its highly laconic statement suggests an apocalypse:

Dove in jay's nest
to rest,
she brides
With an hundred cars.

Dove in jay's nest
at last
and the hundred cars
stand fast. (Ode 12)

In a rendering such as this the effect depends almost entirely upon the tone, and one hardly concerns himself with the allegorical references, except in the most general way. As a matter of fact, the dove (or the bride) does not build its own nest, but occupies, in this case, the jay's (or the groom's); additional specification (for instance, that the lady is to be married to a prince from another state) will add little to the total emotional effect of the rendering, and will perhaps endanger it. Legge takes exception to the orthodox view that the virtue of the bride is being praised, and asserts that the writer was more interested in the splendor of the ceremonies. This may well be so in the original, but it is not so in the reading Pound has given us, which is concerned with the ceremony, not for its material splendor, but for its seemingly mysterious decorum. A clue to the prevailing emotion is, I think, the expression "at last" (not in the original), which suggests a relief psychological, and perhaps metaphysical and moral in its ramifications. It is a counterpart to the experience presented in Ode 1 in which the Prince sought his ideal mate; here, at last, she has been brought home.

There is a difference between panegyric and incantation, between laudatory comparison able to be expressed in verse and semiprophetic utterance that can be sustained only by a poetic idiom. Here, for example, is Waley's translation of the well-known "Peach Tree Ode":

> Buxom is the peach-tree;
> How its flowers blaze!
> Our lady going home
> Brings good to family and house.
>
> Buxom is the peach-tree;
> How thick its leaves!
> Our lady going home
> Brings good to the people of her house.

Pound, eschewing as usual the third person, turns the ode into an apostrophe:

> O omen tree, that art so frail and young,
> so glossy fair to shine with flaming flower;
> that goest to wed
> and make fair house and bower;
>
> O peach-tree thou art fair
> as leaf amid new boughs;
> going to bride;
> to build thy man his house. (Ode 6)

The difference in these two renderings is much more than a matter of craftsmanship. In Waley's—as was intended—we are dealing with an occasional utterance, one that has almost no associative value; in Pound's, we are dealing with sacramental emotion. The peach tree, says one Chinese source, bears fruit earlier than other fruit trees and signifies fertility; it also signifies a beautiful young woman. In addition, Legge informs us that the old critics took the tree, blooming as it does in the spring, as an image that appropriately indicated the bride's adherence to the rite of spring marriage. But only in Pound's version is the image treated as a metaphor, not as a piece of description or a simile. The girl is not *like* a peach tree, she *is* a peach tree, and the decorum of her marriage *is* the harmony of Nature. I might point out, incidentally, that Pound used the epigraph "*kala kagatha*" ("the ideal lady") in its masculine form to describe John Quincy Adams in Canto XXXIII, a strange connection, or perhaps not so strange.[8]

The difference in styles used to achieve the particular effects of the "Dove Ode" and the "Peach Tree Ode" testifies to Pound's abiding need to regard the same material from varying "new angles of vision," or, again, to dramatize it in such a way that it loses its impersonal, repetitious character. Here is his attempt to suggest the formalized emotion associated with the traditional epithalamium:

> Plum flowers so splendid be,
> rolling, onrolling quietly,
> a royal car with young royalty.
>
> Flowers of plum abundantly,
> Heiress of P'ing, heir of Ts'i,
> to their wedding right royally.
>
> Tight as strands in fisherman's line
> may this pair in love combine,
> heir and heiress loyally,
> whereby P'ing is bound to Ts'i. (Ode 24)

Despite the illusion that it gives, this ode is anything but conventional: the metric is irregular, the rhyming occurs on minor accents, and, with the exception of the first two lines of the quatrain, the rhyme scheme is a persistent *a a a,* and so forth. Whatever its irregularities, no ballad, I think, ever looked quite like this one. But the fact is that if Pound were aiming for the effect of decorum, he has been successful. And his success can be ascribed at least in part to the rhyme scheme, which in its uniformity gives an air of discipline to the ode, and in its irregularity precludes the monotony that one could expect to go with it. There is similarly a sense of balance and imbalance in the rhetoric ("rolling, onrolling quietly," "a royal car with young royalty," "heir and heiress loyally"), with one perfect antithesis ("Heiress of P'ing, heir of Ts'i"). But I am belaboring the point. I merely wish to suggest that by the time we reach the line, "whereby P'ing is bound to Ts'i" we are ready to believe it as well as observe it. In a highly wrought lyric that is neither ballad nor epithalamium, Pound has created an emotional illusion associated with both.

Marital life in the *Shih Ching* finds its expression basically in two kinds of odes: of separation, in which the wife, by her response, reveals the qualities of ideal womanhood (loyalty and devotion); and of desertion, in which, by her lament, she exposes the injustices of a harsh world. Other themes appear, such as the bride's nostalgia for her parents and friends (Odes 2, 39, and 59), or the desire for children (Odes 5 and 8), but not with the same frequency, and one soon gets the impression that separation or desertion was both a fact of life and a central moral preoccupation. Only in rare instances is the speaker identified with the husband; it is the fate of the Yin, the passive principle, that becomes an index to the condition of the universe.

The variety of prosodic and rhetorical modes by which Pound renders these themes—a variety that carries with it differences in shades of feeling—makes it hard for us to realize that the originals are of a uniform metric and a more or less consistent rhetoric. Ode 19 is translated in rhyming couplets with a refrain:

> Crash of thunder neath South Hill crest,
> how could I help it, he would not rest,
>   Say shall I see my good lord again?
>
> Crash of thunder under South Hill,
> a fighting man maun have his will,
>   Say shall I see my true lord again?

Like the epithalamium just discussed, this ode is not so regular as it seems, but it does have enough regularity to suggest that it was derived from a song. All the ideas to be stated are stated in the opening stanza, and the ode depends for its effect not on development, but on repetition, with minor variations from stanza to stanza. Yet even within so balladesque and essentially impersonal a form as this ode seems to represent, Pound will still insert informal expressions in the hope of creating a persona: "how could I help it?," "a fighting man maun have his will." The result is that the public form is tempered by the appearance of emotion having a personal quality; and personal emotion, wholly without possibility of development, is defined, made meaningful beyond its mere literal statement, by the ballad form and all that is associated with it. No real depth of sorrow is being (nor is intended to be) expressed here; the prevailing emotion is resignation. Perhaps that is all that the form here used can contain, but it contains it well. Lest one feel that I am doing violence to a simple poem, let me point out that this translation is unique; in most versions, the lady simply expresses longing for her lord and not resignation.

The statement that one yearns for one's husband, even when preceded by an "Oh!," does not necessarily evoke a response from the reader, even when the lady compares her feelings to various conditions in nature. But when an ode of sufficient length allowed for development of the emotions of the speaker, Pound took advantage of his opportunities. The rhetoric and form of Ode 62 evoke the full depth of sorrow of the wife, personal, almost romanticized, in quality. Repetition in the first stanza establishes the tone:

> Baron at arms,
> ten-cubit halbard to war is
> in the front rank
> of the king's forays
>   driving, driving:
> Eastward,
> Eastward.

But it is in the third stanza that the subtleties of the rendering begin to emerge:

Rain, oh rain,
in drought's time,
Or the bright sun quickens;
and a rhyme in my thought of him:
For sweetness of the heart
the head sickens.

In these few lines alone, Pound has made three changes from the original to create a wholly different kind of statement. First, the lady in the Chinese simply compares her condition to a drought; she asks for "rain" but only the "sun" emerges. Pound changes an implied "But" to an "Or" and "emerges" to "quickens" (in the sense of "intensifies," I think), with the result that the utterance comes out not descriptive simile but metaphoric invocation: not "I wish it would rain, but the sun is out"; rather, "Let it rain or else the sun will be too bright (for me to bear)." The significance of this image is clarified by the two changes that follow. The original says, 願 (desire) 言 (particle) 思 (think of) 之 (him); but because 言 is also the radical associated with speaking or writing, we get the remarkable, "and a rhyme in my thought of him." Usually, the last lines are rendered to the effect that the lady's heart is weary (甘 心) with longing, and, as Legge puts it, her "head aches" (首 疾). But Pound has discovered from the Mathews dictionary that the primary meaning of 甘 is not "weary" but "sweet," and with a minor syntactical adjustment gives us, "For sweetness of the heart / the head sickens." The point is that none of these innovations is mechanical or simply a matter of quasi etymology, for from them emerges a single image-complex: the head sickens for sweetness of the heart; the parched mind calls out for rain; the cacophonous thoughts seek "a rhyme." Whereas in the original we have merely the literal assertion of loneliness reënforced by a simile (the drought image)—quite sufficient for a folk song—we have in Pound the linking of disparate elements into a single metaphor or symbol and the consequent creation of poetic utterance.

In the final stanza, Pound completes the development of the metaphor and the emotion:

> How shall I find forgetting-grass
> to plant when the moon is dark
> that my sorrow would pass
> or when I speak my thought? Alas.

There is no dark moon in the Chinese; the word is 背 (*pei,* meaning "behind"—she will plant behind her house). It appears that Pound has erroneously taken the moon from the lower half of the character, mistaking 月, "flesh," for 月, "moon"; furthermore, the top half of the character means "north," not "dark." But the effectiveness of this innovation, aside from its highly evocative quality, comes, I think, from the fact that one can associate it with an internal as well as an external referent. If in one instance the lady's mind is like a bright sun that requires rain, in another it is like a dark moon that requires sun. Finally, the same line that gave us "a rhyme in my thought of him," now is rendered, "when I speak my thought." The syntax of this stanza is confusing but the meaning seems to be that the lady's sorrow will pass when she acquires an herb of forgetfulness or when she can speak her thought, enunciate her feelings. There is then a "rhyme" in her thought of the lord, literally as well as figuratively. The spoken thought of him, the actual rhyme, provides an internal relief or harmony, a rhyme in the heart.

But perhaps I am pushing the imagery too far. In any case, the lady who speaks in Pound's version is far different from the one who speaks in Waley's:

> Heigh, Po [Lord] is brave;
> Greatest hero in the land!
> Po, grasping his lance,
> Is outrider of the king. (Stanza one)

And she concludes her song, "Where can I get a day-lily / To plant behind the house? / All this longing for Po / Can but bring me heart's pain." Perhaps if we could hear her sing, she would not strike us as being quite so superficial.

As I have suggested, despite the consistency of theme and the uniformity of the rhetoric and metric of the original, Pound is at pains to avoid repetition in these odes. Notice the complete difference in tone of:

He's to the war
for the duration;
fowl to their perches,
cattle to byre;
is their food enough;
drink enough
by their camp fire? (Ode 66)

I am hardly maintaining that differences of feeling do not exist among poems of this genre in the original, but rarely, if ever, are there differences in the focus of interest. In the preceding ode, the effect depended wholly on how grief was expressed, not on the fact of its expression. Our attention was directed to the feelings of the speaker, rather than to the situation itself. The lady in this ode is presented to us as the "efficient wife," much more the country girl, who, whatever her emotional capacities, is practical rather than poetic. In short, we are interested in what she says, not the lyrical qualities of her expression. The very form of her utterance precludes emotional depth and what she really elicits is not so much compassion as approval.

In the brief Ode 72 the title is half the poem. Called "Taedium," it is rendered:

Plucking the vine leaves, hear my song:
"A day without him is three months long."

Stripping the southernwoods, hear my song:
"A day without him is three autumns long."

Reaping the tall grass hear my song:
"A day without him's three years long."

Circumscribed by his material, Pound, perhaps self-consciously, affixes the title and bears it out with imitative form. One should keep in mind that this is the version of a poet who will translate repetitions of the same line in the Chinese in such a way that they are rarely recognizable as such. And here our attention is directed neither to the persona nor the situation, but really to the form of the translation, which escapes monotony precisely because it consciously tries to portray it.

In those odes dealing with desertion—or for that matter with separation, too—one occasionally does not know whether he is reading a love poem, a marriage poem, or, in at least one instance, the poem of an officer disaffected from his lord. The problem is inherent in the original and Pound rarely gives any hint of what he thinks the actual subject is, for the yearning of wife for husband can be rendered in no less romantic an idiom than the yearning of a girl for her lover, except that in the former the speaker is sanctioned and in the latter censured by the Confucian interpreters. An abandoned girl or a wife who has not married according to the rites is in large part responsible for her own misery; a deserted wife is usually regarded as the victim of an ill-ruled state, since had the feng of the Prince been correct the husband would have been loyal and the family secure. But these considerations are, as I have said, external to the odes and may or may not have been recognized by Pound.

In odes of this kind, Pound's chief interest was in fashioning a sophisticated and dramatic lament or in creating a complaint that was more than a mere statement of discontent or unhappiness. A wife addresses the sun and moon to witness the mistreatment she receives from her husband and wonders whether his mind will ever become tranquil (rectified) so that he will no longer spurn her. Here is the metamorphosis:

> Sun, neath thine antient roof, moon speaking
> antient speech,
> Bright eyes, shall ye reach the earth, and find
> a man who dwells not in antient right,
> nor shall have calm, putting me from his sight!
> (Ode 29)

No Chinese sun sits beneath an "antient roof" nor do Chinese moons speak "antient speech." Pound has simply taken the expletive 居 literally, 古 meaning old, and 尸 associated with buildings. The expletive 諸 is made into "antient speech" only because of its radical, 言. "Bright eyes" comes from 照, meaning simply "to brighten." But once again this is quasi etymology with a specific metaphorical function. The speaker is doing more than calling on the sun and moon to bear witness to her misery; she is accusing them of being blind to her suffering and tolerant of the man who is causing it:

> shall ye pretend to move
> over the earth
> to find him who returns not my love . . .

Or:

> how should his course run smoothe,
> forgetting love?
>
> . . . .
>
> . . . father and mother mine [sun and moon?]
> that have of me no care,
> shall ye not pine
> that guard not my right!

The sun beneath his ancient roof, the moon speaking ancient speech, are the manifestations of the authority of heaven, and that these "bright eyes" should fail to see the injustice, that these "parents" or ultimate protectors should ignore her plight, is a matter over which there can be no greater despair.

This ode, one will notice, is a much different one from "Moonrise," the lyric discussed earlier in which the speaker identifies his evanescent mistress with the "enquiring moon." The speaker here is not lovesick in the profane sense nor preoccupied with the image of her lover; she is cut off from the universe and her sense of injustice is to be taken seriously—something more than part of a set response. The emotional orientation of this ode has been determined to a large extent by Pound's expanding the sun and moon images the way he has, especially by his use of the highly connotative "antient." Even if this word were wholly devoid of association, its appearance in the two preceding odes would already have prepared the reader for the kind of feeling that Pound is trying to evoke by its use:

> Nor fine nor coarse cloth keep the wind
> from the melancholy mind;
> Only antient wisdom is
> solace to man's miseries. (Ode 27)

And again in the last stanza of the following ode:

> Chung Jen, deep of heart, taught
> me in quietness the antient lordly thought:
> sun's aid, in my littleness.

In this ode, significantly entitled "Limpidity," the grieving speaker is reconciled to the T'ien Ming, or Will of Heaven; the central emotion suggested is that of tranquillity, the profound tranquillity that comes with one's acceptance of the divine order. ("Quietness" becomes a key word for Pound and, not surprisingly, is an innovation; a Chinese singer might have implied but never would have formulated this abstraction.) To return to the ode we have been discussing, I simply mean to point out that the word "antient" ("antient roof," "antient speech," "antient right") does a great deal to establish the speaker's emotion as semireligious, not secular, and to create a much more profound situation than one would normally associate with the pining of a lovesick maid.

Historically, the singer of this ballad is supposedly Chuang Chiang, the neglected wife of a Marquis of Wei. Here is the kind of statement we get from a wife much farther down the social scale:

> Hill-billy, hill-billy come to buy
> silk in our market, apparently?
> toting an armful of calico.

Hill-billy, hill-billy, not at all
but come hither to plot my fall . . . (Ode 58)

The beginning of a marriage that ends in desertion. Hugh Kenner has observed that a Browningesque monologue governs this ode, rendered partly in slang and partly in Elizabethan and Yeatsian idioms.[9] He might also have noticed that the monologue reveals a particular kind of personality, for peasant woman though she may be, the narrator is no clod:

Three years a wife, to work without a roof,
up with the sun and prompt to go to bed,
never a morning off. I kept my word.
You tyrannize, Brothers unaware,
if told would but grin and swear
(with truth, I must confess):
If I'm in trouble, well, I made the mess.

Far from blindly denouncing her husband, the speaker reveals a knowledge of the world she lives in and of her own part in what has happened. The background is that, apparently yielding to a "lustful" man, she married without following the proper rites (so says Legge). Some of the turns of expression that Pound has given her suggest the kind of scepticism and self-knowledge that come with experience: "I went out over the K'i / to Tun Mount, in fact, quite willingly"; "I wept until you came, / trusted your smiling talk. One would." And even, in this innovation, she sounds suspiciously like Pound: "I ever straight / and you ambiguous / with never a grip between your word and act." Her accusation is even-tempered, neither rising to lyric emotion (which would be a violation of her character) nor descending to vituperation—that is her achievement and the achievement of the translator.

Before leaving the subject we might look at a final ode (54), one that, although it is not concerned with desertion, represents the epitome of the sensitive wife victimized by her husband and by a corrupt society: "Baroness Mu impeded in her wish to help famine victims in Wei." One can well imagine what Pound saw in this Chinese situation: a clear-headed wife, with an idea that could be put into action, hampered by weak-minded, bungling authority. Notice the rhetoric of her accusation against her husband:

> Without your visa I could not go,
> I cannot honour your act
> nor retract.
> My sympathy was real, yours the offence
> If I cannot carry my condolence.
> Wrongly you wrought.
> I cannot stifle my thought.

This cold logic, manifest not only in her words but in the very metric of the poem, carries through four stanzas to end in a summary indictment: "All your hundred plans come to naught, / none matched my thought"—a case of inflamed indignation expressing itself in a frozen idiom.

We have no idea whether Pound saw any more in the situation, but the background of this ode makes the moral implications more complex than they appear to be and we might digress for a moment to look at them. The Preface says that the Baroness wanted to return to Wei, her native state, which had recently been overthrown; the famine was a direct result of defeat in battle. The people, led by her brother after the death of the Prince, were "dispersed and living in huts." Mu's state had been too weak to come to their aid. On the other hand, for the Baroness to have returned to Wei would have been a violation of propriety, and her husband's refusal was really based on this point. A conflict of values emerges between what the Confucians might define as *Jen,* Universal Compassion, and *Li,* the Rites. The orthodox solution to this dilemma is not hard to conjecture: Legge tells us that Wei was destroyed by barbarians because it was corrupt, and we can assume that in Confucian thinking it was corrupt because of the decay of royal power. In other words, the situation confronting the Baroness is one that could occur only in a fallen epoch; in a "genuine" epoch she never would have seen her state corrupted and powerless before attackers nor her defeated people destitute, and she never would have been so desperate as to believe that she alone could have saved them:

> I wanted to go to the plains
> where the thick grain is.
> I would have asked of great states,
> their kings and great potentates;
> some would deny, some do their most,
> but I would have had no blame.

Only when we remember the traditional role of women in China (Yin passivity) does the moral problem in this poem really become defined. Rectitude is always victimized in a corrupt state, none more so than that of the sensitive woman in a society in which compassion leads to a violation of propriety and adherence to propriety leads to grief and despair.

5

"Kuo Feng": Men

OF THE various kinds of emotion expressed by men in the "Kuo Feng," the two most distinctive are the longing for home of the soldier and the sorrow of the disaffected scholar or official. As Pound was well aware, war was a, if not *the*, central Confucian preoccupation, and the lament of the soldier was a product and symptom of serious disorder in the universe. The lament of the alienated official speaks for itself and its significance for the translator becomes obvious when we look at some of its forms. Confucius admitted the possibility of two kinds of war: the just, proceeding from the king, and the unjust, proceeding from the vassals. In the former, the military expedition was a defensive instrument used either to quell rebellion or protect the borders from barbarian invasion; its just use as an offensive instrument was possible only upon the foundation of a dynasty sanctioned by heaven, as in the case of Wu Wang, son of Wen. Upon the decline of royal power, war became a result of avarice, and the destruction of the princes who resorted to it, along with the ruin of their people, was inevitable.[1]

Perhaps it occurred to Pound that the lament of the soldier for home was a counterpart of the lament of the lonely wife for her husband. In any case, we find him rendering one such ode in a form almost identical with that in which he rendered a wife's song:

Rapids float no fagot here
nor can she guard Shen frontier.
        Heart, O heart, when shall I home?

(Ode 68)

Recall:

Crash of thunder neath South Hill crest,
how could I help it, he would not rest,
        Say shall I see my good lord again?

(Ode 19)

But like the separation odes centering about a female persona, those of this genre could be rendered in a variety of idioms and with a variety of effects, even when the originals were constructed almost wholly on the principle of repetition rather than development of idea and emotion. Notice what happens in Ode 110, in which the original presents three parallel statements by a father, mother, and brother about the soldier-narrator; as Karlgren renders it: "my father says: Alas, my son has gone out on war service; morning and evening he never stops (working); may he be careful, may he still be able to come, and not remain (there)." The statements of the mother and brother are identical except for minor changes (for instance, "son" is changed to "youngest son" and "younger brother"; "remain (there)" becomes "cast away (there)" and "die (there)"). That these changes are wholly consonant with convention and fully satisfy the Chinese ear is not the issue; the issue is how such minor changes can be translated without banality into English and how monotony can be avoided. Here is Pound's solution:

[Father:] "That boy's on hard service
        days to sundown, no end.
        Let him care for the flag, as I could
            commend.
        So he return in the end."
[Mother:] "No rest, my bairn,
        That his bones lie not in the waste."

[Brother:] "The kid is abroad,
a file filled,
If only he doesn't get killed
(and an eye on the flag.)"

Aside from innovations (such as the flag reference which Pound has gotten from the character 旃, a syntactical particle but defined by Mathews as a "silken banner"), authentic variety is achieved by the use of three levels of idiom, each appropriate to the speaker: the father speaks in a colloquial or normal voice; the mother in a balladesque or poetic voice; and the brother in slang. The result is that the translation emerges as a "playlet" in which actual dramatic tension exists. One may not be entirely satisfied with the brother's statement—among other things, the parenthetical element seems to make it incoherent, unless we are meant to read "and" as though it were "with" and thereby see the full irony of the utterance—but at least one can appreciate Pound's intent.

The attempt to dramatize brief or repetitive odes has, on more than one occasion, led to the creation of new effects with old forms. Here is a version of Ode 36 by Legge:

Reduced! Reduced!
Why not return?
If it were not for your sake, O prince,
How should we be thus exposed to the dew?

The second and last stanza is identical except for the substitution of "person" for "sake" and "mire" for "dew." But this kind of statement has in Pound's mind an English equivalent, and he comes up with:

Why? Why?

By the Lord Wei,
For the Lord Wei this misery
sleeping in dew.
Never pull through!

Sleeping in mud,
why? why?

For Milord Wei.

Is one reminded of:

Pla ce bo,
Who is there? Who?
Di le xi,
Dame Margery.
Fa, re, mi, mi,
Wherefore and why, why?
For the soul of Philip Sparrow,
That was late slain at Carow . . .

But what really makes Pound's use of the Skeltonic line interesting is that here it has been adapted to nonsatiric emotion. Applied to the lament of a soldier, rather than to that of a young girl who has lost her sparrow to a cat, the form generates authentic rather than mock devotional feeling, and the sense of the ridiculous in "For the soul of Philip Sparrow" becomes the sense of high decorum in "For Milord Wei." In a characteristic gesture, Pound entitles the ode "King Charles" and we can assume that the speaker is one of the exiles of his court; the lament is not a true lament but an expression of loyalty: "for no man, but Lord Wei, would we endure such privations." Pound, of course, is not wrenching the Skeltonic form in adapting it to serious purposes; a line capable of mock emotion is equally capable of its heroic counterpart; indeed, its success as a mock form depends upon its ability to suggest heroic emotion.

I persist here because Pound uses the form to render another kind of lament, similar to that of the soldier, in which he attempts to evoke emotion that is even more profound. Thus his version of the song lamenting the voluntary sacrifice of three knights upon the grave of their lord:

Ever unstill, cross, cross,
yellow wings come to the thorn.

Who? with Duke Mu?
Shay Yen-Si. Who?
Shay Yen-Si, pick of an hundred men, shook
at the grave's edge then.
Dark heaven, you take our best men,
An hundred; to have him again. (Ode 131)

The other two knights are lauded in the same fashion.

Yearning for home is emotion serious enough to provide the material for a lyric or a ballad. But Pound was able to find in the soldier, as he found in the wife, a profane as well as a poetic temperament, and once again character or situation rather than tone becomes the center of interest, as in this ode:

Bang the drum. We jump and drill,
some folks are working on Ts'ao Wall
still
or hauling farm loads in Ts'ao
but we're on the roads, south, on the
roads . . .

. . . .

We've rolled 'em flat but
we'll never get home. (Ode 31)

And Pound must have felt that he was indeed resurrecting old China with:

What! no clothes?
My underwear is just your size.
Levies arise,
at the king's call
we rise all
with lances and halbards, together.
(Ode 133)

A rare case of peasant enthusiasm for military life and perhaps natural material for the creation of a persona.

Because the impulse in Pound's version is to lyricize or dramatize, the reader may have little desire to conjecture a meaning beyond the simple antiwar sentiment, and there is little reason to suppose that Pound saw any more in the odes himself, since he was apparently satisfied that that is what Confucius intended by their inclusion in the Anthology. There is, however, something more to the problem. The common soldier was faced with the same kind of dilemma as faced Baroness Mu, a choice between feelings toward the family and duty to authority. When the authority was corrupt (in a "changed" epoch), no genuine resolution was possible and sorrow or despair was the only consequent; as Pound translates in Ode 121, "Such darkness the archèd heaven brings / as the common order of things." On the other hand, participation in a just war, although difficult, was never a cause for despair, since it was characterized by compassion of the king for his men and faith of the men in the king—as in the army of Chou Kung, brother of Wu Wang, who as regent protected the dynasty during an uprising after Wu's death: "He pitied our men," renders Pound, "Yet they were trained. . . . / by his pity of fighting men / they now find rest" (Ode 157). Although taken from their families and homesick after long war, the king's men make no outcry against the injustice of the universe. The logic is understandable enough, but the moral necessity for choosing loyalty to the king over personal feelings has led, in some of the warrior odes of the "Hsiao Ya," to interpretations that will astound the reader of Pound. But we will speak more of that later.

Those odes of the "Kuo Feng" concerned with the disaffection of the official or scholar must have struck Pound with the force of truth, for if the alienation of the honest man in a world of thieves is not a central preoccupation in *The Cantos,* then nothing is. It is true that Pound is not far from a literal rendering when he gives us:

> Rabbit goes soft-foot, pheasant's caught,
> I began life with too much élan,
> Troubles come to a bustling man.
> "Down Oh, and give me a bed!" (Ode 70)

But when one recalls the personal references in the *Pisan Cantos*—for example, "There is fatigue deep as the grave," and especially, "Down, Derry-down / Oh let an old man rest" (Canto 83), one can sense more than an objective interest in this ballad. The persona here is no official, as Legge says it is, but is the troubadour himself.[2]

The irony is that Pound is not always successful with this genre in the "Kuo Feng" and he is often conspicuously unsuccessful with it in the "Hsiao Ya." Part of the difficulty comes, I think, from uncertainty whether to render in a casual or an elevated idiom, an uncertainty reflecting contradictory images of the poet in Pound's own mind. Or perhaps it is simply that his ear detected no discordance in the juxtaposition of poetic diction and slang. An interweaving, seemingly deliberate, appears, for instance, in Ode 40 in which the opening line is "North gate, sorrow's edge," an elevated statement followed by "purse kaput, nothing to pledge." And the third line, "I'll say I'm broke," is succeeded by a line that should (but does not) move toward lyrical suggestivity, "none knows how, heaven's stroke." The problem is clarified in the next stanza:

> When I go back where I lived before,
> my dear relatives slam the door,
> This is the job put up on me,
> Sky's "which and how"?
> or say: destiny.

Here we have sarcasm on the one hand and an inarticulate attempt at lyricism on the other. One is so distracted by the triteness and ineptitude of the language that the ultimate meaning of the ode, the acceptance by the narrator of the Will of Heaven and his resignation to his fate, is of little consequence.

A similar ode, 65, Pound thought important enough to ascribe a title ("Thru the Seasons"), an epigraph (" 'O thou man.' Thos. Hardy in Under the Greenwood Tree"), and a postscript (" 'Tous je connais' / Villon"), and to provide an alternative reading. But the paraphernalia does not conceal the uncertainty of the translation:

> Black millet heeds not shaggy sprout,
> Aimless slowness, heart's pot scraped out,
> Acquaintance say: Ajh, melancholy!
> Strangers: he hunts, but why?
> Let heaven's far span, azure darkness,
> declare what manner of man this is.

The rendering is sabotaged by expressions like "aimless slowness," the almost ludicrous, "Ajh, melancholy," and the banal, "he hunts, but why?," to say nothing of the distortion, "Acquaintance say." The alternative is even worse than the original:

> Straggling millet, grain in shoot,
> aimless slowness, heart's pot scraped out,
> acquaintance say: He is melancholy;
> Strangers: what is he hunting now?
>   Sky, far, so dark.
>   "This, here, who, how?"

In the almost identical Ode 109, Pound manages one lyrical line ("as my worry goes into song") before giving us such dialogue as, "Strangers say: 'The scholar is proud. / Others fit in. Why's he so loud?' " But there is no need to extend the discussion. The ideogrammic method has its weaknesses, serious ones.

Pound's greatest success in treating the alienated moralist comes in the four odes of Kuei (Odes 146–149). The original of Ode 146 is a straightforward indictment of the ruler by the poet as rendered by Legge (but is sufficiently ambiguous to be treated as an ode of yearning by Waley and Karlgren):

> In your lamb's fur you saunter about;
> In your fox's fur you hold your court.
> How should I not think anxiously about you?
> My toiled heart is full of grief.

Pound follows Legge, but he turns direct statement into mockery:

> Fine clothes for sport
> And slops in court

and your intent
is to show talent
for government?

(The Lord is clearly seen here as having violated propriety by wearing the wrong clothes on state occasions.) The last line in Legge's translation, above, is a refrain that appears after each of the three stanzas in the ode, but, with a deliberate use of anticlimax that is highly effective, Pound holds it back until the end of the poem:

Sure, the wool shines like fat
in the sun's rays; reflects the light
and is quite scintillant,
feathers of light in fact
to my heart's blight.

But it is in Ode 147 that Pound reaches the highest lyrical level we can expect to find in this genre; here the alienated speaker imagines finding someone who, by obeying the funeral rites for parents, displays filial piety:

Saw I a white cap now,
it were as music mid thorns,
Haro! the day.

Saw I white knee-pads decent misery
I'd know one man still feels and thinks as I.

By this time the reader can guess what image is quasi-etymological, and furthermore he will be little surprised to learn that "Haro! the day" is Pound's equivalent for "toiled heart," which appeared in the ode discussed a moment ago.

Actually, many of the niceties of the translation might still be easily overlooked. In Ode 148, Legge tells us, the speaker, oppressed by the government, wished he had the unconsciousness of a tree, a traditional interpretation disputed by modern scholarship. Pound follows this view, except for Legge's identification of the tree as a "carambola";

Vitex in swamp ground,
branched loveliness,

would I could share that shrub's unconsciousness.

Vitex negundo, casting thy flowers in air . . .

Pound's Latin designation is not only more euphonious, but more meaningful (Denier of Life?).[3] Whether or not the original expresses a death wish, the rendering does so in tone as well as statement.[4]

The final ode in the sequence is called "The Kettle-Drums," and since it has nothing whatsoever to do with kettle drums we are directed to see Frobenius, who has noted that such drums "were made for temporary use by stretching the cover over nomad's pots." It does not take much imagination to see what Pound is driving at, for the speaker himself is a nomad drumming out an epitaph of Chou on its ruined highways:

Not the wild wind
nor the roar of the chariots
    But the ruin of Chou's way
    breaks me.

. . . .

If a man would home West
let him cherish this tone.

Panegyrics, satires, and occasional odes make up the remainder of the "Kuo Feng," but it would be foolish to dismiss them with mere mention of their themes. The panegyric to the Lord, like the epithalamium, depended wholly on the sense of decorum for its effect, since it represented a public and externalized emotion and could not be rendered in terms of a persona. Furthermore, the originals were rarely specific enough to define character with precision; their praise was the kind appropriate to song, filled with expletives, forthright comparisons, laudatory formulae, and unornamented description. Similarly, as in panegyrics in any language, the sources of praise were standardized and limited; the good Lord was an imitation of Wen Wang or, more simply, a just ruler, a great builder of cities, or a loyal warrior. I should add that one's belief that he is reading a panegyric as panegyric is often contingent upon the Confucian interpretation. For instance, Pound's

> Such subtle prince is ours
> to grind and file his powers
> as jade is ground by wheel;
> he careth his people's weal . . . (Ode 55)

may strike the reader as being perfectly straightforward. But Legge gives us merely,

> There is our elegant and accomplished
>   prince,—
> As from the knife and the file,
> As from the chisel and the polisher!
> How grave is he and dignified!

and Waley sees nothing political at all in the ode; the speaker becomes a lady admiring not the character but the features of her lord:

> As thing cut, as thing filed,
>
> . . . .
>
> Oh, the grace, the elegance!

Pound's reading is based on the Confucian notion of self-rectification, and the epigraph ("polumetis," of many counsels) identifies the lord with Odysseus.

Aiming as it does at a sense of decorum and, perhaps, a sense of discipline corresponding to the subject, the rhetoric of Pound's translation is based on a series of parallel laconic statements that maintain the repetitive quality of the original. For example, the last lines of stanza one,

> stern in attent,
> steady as sun's turn bent
> on his folk's betterment
>   nor will he fail.

are matched in the last lines of the second stanza with the same alliteration: "splendid, steadfast in judgement-hall / he cannot fail us / nor fall." Not until the last lines of the final stanza does Pound break the parallelism with an etymological translation in which the prince is made to "lean / over chariot rail in humour / as he were a tiger / with velvet paws." Whatever its violation of the original, an image like this one lends considerable color to the English and, indeed, the panegyric is a mode that can use whatever color is given to it.

The use of laconic syntactical parallels also appears in the ode on the Ting Star in which the hero is praised as a builder of cities (Ode 50), but, as a device of narration rather than static description, it infuses the poem with epic emotion:

> The star of quiet being in mid-sky,
> he reared up Bramble hall;
> took sun to measure the wall;
> planted abundantly
> chestnut and hazel tree;
> tung tree and varnish roots
> whence wood to make our lutes.[5]

There is little doubt that this idiom does exactly what Pound wants it to do, for it raises the catalogue of activity to poetry. The only trouble is that Pound's ear detects no discrepancy in lines like "learned from the shell what was eventually, / that is, the event in its probity," nor the debilitating distortion of rhyme in "so straight a man, the course / of heart so deep / that gave him three thousand tall horse."

The rhetorical modes available for the praise of men are, of course, as numerous as those available for the praise of women. Aside from the kind of statement represented by "Polumetis" and its epic equivalent in Ode 50, we have the balladesque song of the enigmatic Ode 11 in which a "mythical beast" of supernatural gentleness is identified with Wen, the pure balladesque of Ode 130 ("The outdoor chief establishes court"), and even the lyrical reverie of Ode 128 in which a lady imagines the figure of her warrior husband, "neat as jade" in her "thought confused." In this last poem the lady announces that she is engaged in reverie, and the long lines interspersed in her speech actually create the dreamlike quality, the sense of reverie, that lies beyond actual statement. Thus while the original is a simple panegyrical song, the translation is a lyrical vision:

So have I seen him in his service car
who now in war afar,
five bands on the curving pole, side shields
and silver'd trace,
bright mats and bulging hub;
dapple and white-foot pace
into my thought. I see him neat as jade
in service shack, and in my thought confused.

The words themselves are a close approximation of the original; it is their particular arrangement—their rhythm—that has created the psychological effect. In one way the ode is a counterpart to Ode 1 in which the Prince, dreaming of his mate, really seemed to be dreaming.

Panegyrics that have peasant figures or artisans as the subjects, like other odes that have them as subjects, do not aim at the elevated emotion found in odes to aristocratic figures. From the literary point of view, the statement of praise does not suggest any feeling beyond itself; the image of the good man is presented in a colloquial diction that seeks, sometimes successfully, sometimes not, to engage the reader by its vitality. Thus the rabbit catcher in Ode 7:

Deep in mid forest pegging the nets,
elegant in his art;
fit to be the duke's confidant,
His very belly and heart.

The gamekeeper in Ode 25:

Of five young wild pig he shoots but one,
Green grow the rushes, oh!

White-Tiger is a true forester's son.

Shu, the hunter, in Odes 77 and 78:

Shu goes hunting, no one stays
in the town's lanes and by-ways
or if they do
there's not a he-man there like Shu.[6]

Or the soldier in Ode 80:

Note that lamb coat, fleecy to leopard cuff,
a dude, but he knows his stuff.

Just as in the original the panegyrics are direct in their praise, so the odes of censure are direct in their exposure, and the use of a satiric idiom is wholly the choice of the translator. Some of the characteristics of Pound's satiric style have already been noted, but there is really not much to examine, for Pound time and again draws on a limited number of devices: the mock Latin phrase ("*id est*, Miss Ts'i shooting the moon," or "clearly with naught to learn *in feminis*"); the pun ("if you take not the pin's point, but ours"); the ironic statement set off in quotations ("a 'button man,' came to administer / and have charge of the public roads"); and the obviously ironic or sarcastic statement ("and, loose on Lu Road, Miss Ts'i / showing compassion abundantly"). Whatever the "liveliness" these devices inspire, Pound is not at his best in this idiom either as a poet or translator, or perhaps it would be better to say that the final product does not always justify the liberties taken with the original. Ode 108 in which the officer of an invading army is censured by the people for seeking petty profit at their expense provides us with this example:

By one crook of the Fen ox-lip grows
that Fen folk once gathered to ease their woes
till we got such a gem of an officer
of the Duke's household,
of the kind some dukes prefer.

In the original the officer is actually conceded to be as elegant as a gem because of his ornate clothing, and I admit there is no little cleverness in Pound's rendering this statement "till we got such a gem of an officer." The trouble is that the expression is trite and the "Americanization" blatant and heavy handed, a metamorphosis that is neither faithful to the Chinese "spirit" nor effective as independent satire.

I am perhaps being too severe in this particular instance but Pound is clearly addicted to the use of ironic expressions that are either inconsistent with their context or ineffectual. A guardsman, misemployed as a ballet dancer by his corrupt lord (Ode 38), is made to express his feelings as though he were indeed sophisticated: "West Country men for prettiness, who guessed? / What ass would say: this beauty's from the West?" (Pound apparently favors the term "ass," since it appears again uttered by a peasant girl: "But play the pretentious ass again, and / some other young captain will do." Ode 87.) And here is the voice of a maiden satirizing the lover who has spurned her, in the poem Pound calls "Wolf" (slang): "Should we melt / at the flap of his sash ends? . . . / we will not, I think, melt, (complacency in its *apogee*) / at the flap of his sash ends" (Ode 60). Is a rhyme like, "This fellow's beneath the rat's modus, / why delay his exodus," (Ode 52) incisively funny or simply ludicrous?

I am aware that Pound may think that he is imitating the satiric techniques of Jules Laforgue, of whom he has written, "He deals for the most part with literary poses and *clichés,* yet he makes them a vehicle for the expression of his own personal emotions, of his own unperturbed sincerity." As an example, he cites this passage from "Pierrot (*Scène courte, mais typique*)": "*Je ne suis pas 'ce gaillard-la!' ni Le Superbe! / Mais mon âme, qu'un cri un peu cru exacerbe, / Est au fond distinguée et franche comme une herbe.*" [7] But theory notwithstanding, it is clear, even in this brief example, that Laforgue is much better at the game. Pound is a lyric poet, not a formidable satirist.

Actually, the most interesting aspect of the odes of

censure is not the emotion with which Pound has invested them but their implications to the Confucian mind. Consider, for instance, the officer of the invading army in Ode 108. Because he is an invader, his character is determined; his elegance is not true elegance, "neat as jade," but the spurious one of vanity. His clothes belie his actual pettiness; he not only violates the decorum of his rank by gathering sorrel, but does so in such a way that the people suffer, since he deprives them of a source of profit. There are, of course, worse crimes, but in Confucian thought no transgression is a thing in itself; an officer gathers sorrel because he has no sense of decorum; he has no sense of decorum because he has no moral guidance; he has had no guidance because his Prince is corrupt—as evidenced by his militance. The character of the ruler, the society, and the times can be read in the apparently minor crime. If the vassal is a petty profiteer, so is the ruler, as Ode 107, a complaint by the ruler's wife (?), would suggest:

> Thin fibre shoes 'gainst frost,
> At soft hands' cost a girl can make her clothes
> or ply the needle with those same hands
> To make her goodman's stiff belt and bands.
> Goodman? or mean? we mean
> good to accumulate and accumulate . . .

Accordingly, in the remaining odes the general conditions in the state are revealed: the avarice of the nobility and the resentment of the people, for a man who will pilfer sorrel will pilfer considerably more:

> RATS,
> stone-head rats lay off our grain,
> three years pain,
> enough, enough, plus enough again.
>
> (Ode 113)

The hunters in Ode 97 who are censured for their false courtesy, the courtier in Ode 100 forced to attend an audience in the middle of the night because the ruler is unaware of the proper rites, the misemployed guard, and the complaining maiden all provide insights into the world they inhabit, and, consequently, a moral revelation to the reader. Once again, we have no way of knowing whether Pound saw these implications or whether he saw only the historical model for the petty usurer.

I have discussed in detail Pound's reading of the major genres of the "Kuo Feng" because it is in these poems that his measure as a translator, poet, and interpreter is clearly revealed. The same virtues and deficiencies carry over, generally, into the treatment of the "Ya" and "Sung," but Pound's specific solution to the problems presented by these odes is still worth examining, for here we are faced with relatively long, semi-didactic poems that would be a challenge to any translator. As one might well imagine by now, Pound's achievements and failures in this medium are equally conspicuous.

6

"Ya" and "Sung": State and Heaven

In the Confucian mind, the central political relationship was that of the king and his vassals, for strict adherence to even the pettiest of distinctions in the hierarchy of power was the sole human guarantee of harmony in the state, and the sole means for acknowledging the order of heaven. This principle lies behind the whole eight decads of the "Hsiao Ya," the so-called "Minor Elegantiae," which are minor only in the sense that they are concerned with the affairs of state rather than of heaven (that is, with administration rather than the foundation of dynasty) and elegant only in the sense that they represent the moral refinements designed to illuminate the listener.[1] If originally the "Kuo Feng" was a collection of folk songs, the "Ya," it is believed, was a collection of ceremonials—songs actually sung on the occasions appropriate to their subjects—and complaints against the royal fall from virtue. In Confucian terms, the feng (influence) received by the people and manifested in the folk songs now becomes the ya (principle of rectification) emanating from the king and manifested in the official songs.

According to the historical reading, the collection centers about the Chou kings, both good and evil, who represent a decline from the golden age (the eras of Wen, Wu, and Ch'eng, 1184–1079 B.C.). In the "changed" epoch, which spanned several centuries, rulers were a mixture of virtue and corruption, such as Hsuan Wang (827–782 B.C.), who began his reign in the image of Wen and ended in dissolution, or they were wholly without virtue, such as Li Wang (878–842 B.C.) and Yu Wang (780–771 B.C.), who was the last and perhaps most corrupt of the Western Chou. Odes that appear in the first two and a half decads ("Deer Sing," "White Flower," and "Red Bows") are considered "cheng," as having originated in the time of Wen; the remainder are "pien," either reflecting degenerated customs or "nostalgically" harking back to the old era. If one is to talk of recapturing the spirit of the originals, then, one must speak of the demand in both instances (ceremonial and complaint) for elevation of emotion and dignity. The festival odes, for example, which constitute the chief ceremonial genre of the section, are far from being merely songs of revel. They are actually songs of decorum, for the feast was the public embodiment of ceremony, an activity designed to symbolize the existence of the hierarchy and the proper relations between king and vassal. The multitude of regulations prescribed for each step in the progress of the feast had the single aim of making the participant aware of his place and of eliciting from him the proper emotions in regard to superiors and inferiors. The very existence of a banquet held in accordance with the Chou Rite was symptomatic, so the Confucians believed, of a well-ordered society. Since the festival was held to honor ministers and vassals, through it the king revealed that he was surrounded by virtuous men who deserved reward, and their general submission to the Rite was the external manifestation of the heart rectified by his feng (or ya). These odes also have attached to them the mystique of a fertility (abundance) celebration, since the righteousness of the king and agricultural productivity were thought to be directly related. As for the complaints, they are the most numerous in the book and generally center about the breakdown in relations between king and minister, characterized by the alienation of honest men and the rise to power of slanderers, flatterers, or favorite concubines, the rejection of legitimate heirs and legal wives, or the general failure to obey the old rites. But the aim of the complaint is not so much to denounce as to exhort or to persuade directly or indirectly. The point becomes almost self-evident when one realizes that the king, no matter how corrupt, was still the Son of Heaven, and the minister, no matter how righteous, was bound to a certain amount of awe.

In rendering these odes (and the "Great Ya" and "Sung" as well), the translator whose interests are literary rather than sociological has the heavy burden of providing variety and interest to, as well as intimating depth of emotion in, what is essentially a large body of didactic, functional, and repetitious poetry. Pound tried to solve this problem by using the same techniques that he used in rendering the folk songs, namely those that would "lyricize" or "colloquialize" the material and give the illusion of a person speaking. This solution fails, I think, not because it is in theory unsound, but once again because of Pound's utter lack of talent in handling the colloquial idiom and his indiscriminate fluctuation between genuine and false voices. Even if the point be conceded that great liberty can be taken with an original to achieve literary quality, a large number of Pound's versions still do not stand as independent poems.

Consider, for instance, the sequence of festival odes that includes the "Deer Cry" and "White Flower" decads. First, let it be said that Pound is fully capable of rendering an ode that is wholly in harmony with the original and has poetic merit as well. The "nobles reply to one of the . . . 'Deer Odes' " (Ode 166) is one such example:

Heaven conserve thy course in quietness,
Solid thy unity, thy weal endless
that all the crops increase and nothing lack
in any common house.

But the handling of the ode to which this is the reply is more characteristic. We begin, confidently enough, in the realm of the mysterious:

> "Takk! Takk!" axes smack
> Birds sing "ying, ying"
> . . . .
>
> . . . .
> Spirits attend
> him who seeketh a friend.
> Air, hear our cry
> concording harmony.

This highly effective rendering is followed by a passage that in both diction and rhythm plummets us back into what Pound thinks is reality but is actually inanity:

> . . . I call all
> my dad's clan, if they come not, not
> my fault, they were invited, all hereabout.
>
> . . . .
>
> None of my mother's folk have been slighted,
> If they don't come they were, in any case,
> invited.

Or here is an example of Pound trying to raise a tankard, one that proves heavy indeed:

> South lakes full of flickering fish,
> Barbel makes a pretty dish,
> jab down that top-net on 'em!
> A gent by liquor gets good guests,
> blessings upon 'em! (Ode 171)

An ode like "Fraternitas," with its mixture of lyric diction and cliché, seems to be a deliberate travesty of all poetic expectations. The title itself lends a certain amount of dignity and in fact the tone appears to be solemn:

> Splendour recurrent
> in cherry-wood,

in all the world there is
nothing like brotherhood.

(Ode 164)

Even here we have a cliché, although it is mild in comparison to the ones that follow: "in a pinch," " 'short of brute force' " "stew / in their own juice," and so forth. Perhaps Pound is attempting to raise a banal diction into poetic statement by sheer force of tone and rhythm, a way of thinking dating back to his days as an imagist. But I am not convinced that the poetic can justify the poem.

The same general reasoning probably lies behind the somewhat more successful version of the first ode in the "Hsiao Ya." Perhaps with Frobenius's kettle drums still in mind, Pound gives us this reading:

"Salt
lick!" deer on waste sing,
k'in plants for tasting, guests to feasting;
beat drum and strumm [sic]
lute and guitar,
lute and guitar to get
deep joy where wine is set
'mid merry din
let the guest in, in, in, let the guest in.

The innocuous-seeming "beat drum" comes from Pound's direct interpretation of 鼓, which usually means drum but in the combination 鼓瑟 means to play the lute. Apparently this view is responsible for the drum-beat rhythm that seems to underlie the ode. Whether one is convinced by this exercise in imitative form is perhaps a matter of personal taste. As noisy as the last line might seem, Pound was, I think, trying to suggest a ritual air to the event. His version of a non-ritualistic feast needs no comment:

Guests start eatin', mild and even,
The sober sit an' keep behavin',
but say they've booz'd then they do not.
When they've booz'd they start a-wavin' an'
a-ravin',

> Yas' sir they rise up from the ground
> And start dancin' an' staggerin' round. (Ode 220)

Of the dozens of odes of complaint that constitute the "Ya," a few examples will be sufficient to give the measure of Pound's performance in this medium. Ode 191, for example, is a characteristic attack by an honest official upon a minister of Yu Wang (780–771 B.C.), who plays a large role in the "Hsiao Ya" as the very embodiment of royal corruption. Still, the kind of attack made in the original is not at all like that made in the translation—and the difference is revealing. In the original, the emotional tension depends on a contrast between the minister, Lord Yin's, high position and his evildoing, a contrast that "baffles" the speaker, since it should naturally be assumed that high position and rectitude are inseparably bound. Thus Karlgren renders:

> Crest-like is that Southern mountain; its rocks are massed high; oh, majestic Master Yin, the people all look at you; the grieved hearts are as if burning, they dare not jest or chat; the state is entirely . . . destroyed . . . why do you not make a scrutiny?

Like the pine, cypress, or bamboo, the mountains are traditionally associated with the Lord in his moral as well as social and political role. This distinction, crucial to the original, is ignored by Pound who uses the images not as emblems of augustness (even pseudo respect) but as emblems of pride:

> Abacus against high cloud, crag over crag,
>   Mount South
> to echo with cry on cry;
> O'er-towering Yin, thou proud
> as people cower, burning with inner heat
> daring no open jest, so soon an end,
> the hour all-seen, save in thy mind.

("Abacus" is used here in its architectural sense, "the top of a column.") After beginning with this kind of comparison, Pound was forced to use it throughout the succeeding stanzas. In the original we have, "Crest-like is that Southern mountain, full is its richness (of vegetation) . . . Oh Grand-master Yin, you should be the base of Chou." All of this is meant quite literally. But Pound says:

> Grade over grade, Mount South,
> so thick thy gnarl of wood,
>
> . . . .
>
> Yin, viceroy
> "foundation stone" of Chou . . .

Pound has had to resort to quotation marks to show that the expression was, in his opinion, being used ironically. I am not pointing out these differences just for their own sake; they are suggestive of the abyss between the attitudes of a man like Pound aspiring to use Chinese values and those of a Chinese expressing those values. The aim of the original is indeed to rectify, not just condemn, to recall the minister to his name and position so that they will have true meaning and the foundation of the state will be firm. Pound's aim is simply to condemn or to achieve a general ironic effect, and there is an unmistakable impression that whereas the Chinese has every impulse to reëducate the criminal, Pound has every impulse to destroy him. No matter how contemptible the ruler, the author of the ya of resentment still felt some kind of identity with the regime, for revolution was a course to be followed only by those virtuous enough to be endowed with the Ming of Heaven, not just the victims of the emperor's corruption. That was the very *raison d'être* of the ya of resentment; it was the accepted instrument of the oppressed for making the blind ruler aware of his environment. In a world in which no man dared "an open jest," the writer of the ya could express criticism and even mention his name (in this case Chia-fu) with impunity. If the king failed to heed the criticism, heaven itself might warn him by allowing mountains to crumble and by bringing drought and famine. For an avant-garde Western moralist, whether the judged be men of the past or present, rectification extended only to the reader, and then only in the vague sense that he should be made aware of what were supposedly the moral realities of history. He was expected to hate the villain and exalt the hero. True, Kung had the same expectations of those who were exposed to the *Shih,* but to him education was aimed at the Lord himself and led to moral evolution. For Pound, as is suggested by his ill-concealed irony and often blatant vituperation, education could lead to nothing less than the desire to overthrow an enslaving authority that was beyond rectification and with which Pound publicly repudiated any identification whatsoever.

Pound's tendency to impose his own conception of morality upon the Chinese—or, conversely, to interpret Chinese values solely in terms of his own under the theory of "equivalents"—is general throughout the "Ya." Furthermore, while it is his aim to "modernize" and dramatize his material, he is capable of doing so only in a limited way. Ode 193, for example, is concerned with another of Yu's ministers:

> Hwang-Foo is very wise;
> He has built a great city for himself in Hëang.
> He chose three men as his ministers,
> All of them indeed of great wealth.
> He could not bring himself to leave a single
> minister,
> Who might guard our king. (Legge)

As I take it, the point here is to indicate a hierarchal disorder in Yu's reign, with the example of a minister usurping the prerogatives of the ruler by building for himself a great city. Pound's reading is,

> Our prudent Huang has had a building scheme
> And three contracting lords are now enriched,
> There's no police chief left for royal guard,
> the hunting set has been, all, led Hiang-ward.
> (To Huang's new town, that is.)

One can easily see what has happened here: the minister has become corrupt in a petty way, giving out contracts and taking bribes. But the issue in the original is not petty corruption, it is usurpation, and the sin is not avarice but pride. The latter is far more serious because it suggests more than just a common political malaise; it suggests the positive defiance of heaven. Only when this fact is appreciated does the eclipse mentioned in the first stanza of the ode become meaningful. The irony, then, is not that Huang is a corrupt and inefficient planner and that the narrator "dare not post a monthly works report, / knowing the mare's-nest it would raise in court," but that Huang is all too efficient. His image is that of a vassal rising to power and challenging the central authority, the prototypical satanic situation that, in Confucian thought, is the cause of all national woe.

Incidentally, there is another moral aspect to this ode, one that Pound seems to have appreciated. "Of Queen Pao Sy," his introduction reads, "Huang's town planning at Hiang, and the Solar Eclipse of 29 August 776 B.C." Pao Sy (Pao Ssu) was a concubine who virtually enslaved Yu Wang in characteristic violation of the natural order of heaven (the Yin dominating the Yang). In other words, even though she is scarcely mentioned, Pao Ssu is the true subject of the poem, since she is the cause of Yu's deterioration and his deterioration makes the success of overweening ministers possible. As revealed in the *Cantos*, Pound has taken up the judgment that women in general, along with eunuchs, were *the* pernicious influence in Chinese dynastic history, a general Confucian appraisal that did not necessarily require an understanding of or involvement in the complex feudal attitudes of which it was a part.

These odes are a fair indication of what one can expect from Pound throughout the "Hsiao Ya." When he chooses to use a consistently lyrical idiom he can produce a genuine equivalent, as in Ode 175 ("Red Bows"), in which the emotion is the sense of decorum, not hilarity or the sense of good fellowship. The lyric idiom is no guarantee, however, that the spirit of the original will be recaptured. Odes like 162 and 163, for instance, in which the subject is the weary but loyal soldier and the conscientious legate seeking information about the condition of the empire, are actually ceremonial songs prescribed in the *I Li* (*Book of Ceremony*). But Pound is interested not in recapturing their ceremonial aura so much as in creating a vivid sense of the exhaustion of the speakers, and especially in Ode 163 he uses a rhythm imitative of speed and exhaustion. Translations of this kind are really no problem, for at worst they succeed as independent poems, and that justifies a great deal. It is when they do not succeed as independent poems that the translations, if accurate, are no better than those of other translators—since Pound is bringing to them no special knowledge of the language—and, if inaccurate, are a futile drain on the reader's sensibilities. Even if one were to accept many of Pound's devices for creating personae in the folk songs, one must inevitably begin to find them cloying in the ya. When he abandons the one idiom in which he is secure, all personae seem to coalesce. A nobleman or a commoner, a king or peasant, speak like midwestern Americans are supposed to speak, not only because it is Pound's theory that they should do so, but because he does not have the resources to recapture a variety of idioms.

Further, unlike Hugh Kenner, I see little change in quality, for instance, between the version of Ode 167 that appeared in *Cathay* ("Song of the Bowmen of Shu") and the present one, although it is clear that a dramatizing process has been at work.[1] Granted, the early reading was prosaic: "Here we are, picking the first fern-shoots / And saying: When shall we get back to our country? / Here we are because we have the Ken-nin for our foeman, / We have no comfort because of these Mongols." And it is true that the later version, at least in the first few stanzas, seems to have the rhythm of a marching song:

> Pick a fern, pick a fern, ferns are high,
> "Home," I'll say: home, the year's gone by,
> no house, no roof, these huns on the hoof.
> Work, work, work, that's how it runs,
> We are here because of these huns.

But if this reading is dramatically superior to the earlier one, it is still too contrived to be really effective; one is not convinced that he is listening to a soldier—modern American or ancient Chinese. And it was the boy from Philadelphia, not Hailey, Idaho, who wrote these lines: "Yaller bird, let my corn alone, / Yaller bird, let my crawps alone, / These folks here won't let me eat / I wanna go back whaar I can meet / the folks I used to know at home" (Ode 187). The original perhaps calls for dialect, since the Confucian reading is that it represents the deterioration of human relations among the peasantry as a direct result of royal corruption, but Pound's reply, energetic though it may be, is something less than satisfactory.

From the three decads of the "Ta Ya" there emerges a single Chinese preoccupation, that of the revelation of the T'ien Ming in the ultimate realm of human affairs: the founding and maintenance of a dynasty. If the "Kuo Feng" is concerned with the relations between man and wife and the "Hsiao Ya" with those between king and vassal, the "Ta Ya" is concerned with the relation between the king and heaven. Specifically, the revelation of the Ming of Heaven is manifest in the rise of the Chou, whose history begins in myth and ends in fact. The triumph of Wu, son of Wen, and the very embodiment of virtue in a lord, over Chou Hsin, the degenerate king and last of the Shang (or Yin) Dynasty, is the prototypical example of the way in which the mind of heaven works, and becomes in Confucian thought the admonition par excellence to all succeeding rulers.

In the celebration of Wen, the father, who died eleven years before Wu succeeded in overthrowing the Shang (1122 B.C.), lies the essential difference between the Western and the Chinese approach to the epic experience. During his lifetime, Wen never assumed the title of "Wang," king, an example of *cheng ming* indicative of his virtue. He was known as the "Chief of the West," a title that did not conflict with the king's. His deference to the ruler, be that ruler degenerate or not, was clearly, in Confucian thought, one of the bulwarks of his virtue; and reflected in his glorification is the Confucian obsession with the profound illegality of any kind of attack by a vassal upon the royal position. Wen makes known his outrage at some of the atrocities committed at the court by Chou Hsin and is imprisoned for three years as a potential revolutionary; refusing to escape, he tells his sympathizers, "When a child is not loved by a father, he does not for that reason alone stop obeying and respecting him; merely because a subject disapproves of the conduct of his king, he has no right to fail in his loyalty." [2] After his restoration, Wen does participate in wars of tranquilization against vassals in whose states conditions have become unbearable to the people. His own state is sufficiently utopian to shame two quarreling lords, who have come to Chou for arbitration, into leaving without seeing him and into broadcasting his virtues throughout the kingdom.

It is left to Wu to make the actual conquest of the Shang, and paradoxically for this very reason he does not have the moral stature of his father, or in any case he is regarded as his father's son, rather than as a hero in his own right. Eleven years after Wen's death, Wu finally takes action, a reluctance perhaps exasperating to a Western reader but not without Chinese moral logic. Regarded from a purely political point of view, the poems of the first two decads, as H. G. Creel perceptively points out, might simply be the attempt of the Chou kings to establish legitimacy; from a Confucian point of view they alleviate the moral burden of Wu's revolt: he is but a "little child," as he says during the speech at Mu before the battle, and by that I assume he means that he is but the amoral implement of heaven. It is not the will of the Chou clan that the king be deposed, but the will of heaven, a heaven that acts through its most virtuous subjects to rid itself of a king by whom it has been affronted.

The epic poetry of the *Shih*, purely moral as it is, has led Max Weber to suggest that the collection may indeed have been edited by Confucius; unlike the Western epic, it does not celebrate the warrior-hero nor dwell upon his deeds.[3] In other words, its interest is in revelation, not plot, in the supremacy of heaven, not in human glory. The true hero exists before the story begins and the conqueror, the man of action, forswears his role, for only in such denial is salvation possible.

The "Ta Ya," then, has neither historical nor literary continuity—that is, it cannot be read with the same expectations one has in reading a Western epic. Rather, it follows the same plan that characterizes the "Kuo Feng" and the "Hsiao Ya": all of the first decad ("Wen Wang") and six poems of the second ("Sheng Min" or "Birth of the People") are the cheng odes that establish the moral ideal and represent the manifestation of the Ming of Heaven in the affair of dynasty; the last four odes of the "Sheng Min" and all of the concluding decad, "T'ang," are pien, and represent the perversion of the ideal. Specifically, the aim is to establish the continuity of virtue in the Chou clan from Wen backward to a mythical ancestor (Hou Tsi, a semidivine figure of fertility) and forward, prophetically, to Wen's descendents and successors. Since the Chou clan and the people of Chou are one, family and national virtue are identical; not only are the actual kings who follow Wen to be rectified, but so are the officers of the state and the subjects themselves. Wen thus emerges in the first ode as a spirit comprehended in terms of light and therefore representing the principle of Yang among men. His brilliance is merely another metaphor for his feng, moral force, which is exerted through both time and space.

Among the subjects of the odes, then, aside from the central one of Wu's victory on the plains of Mu, are Tai Sze, wife of Wen, "a younger sister of heaven" (Ode 236), Chi-Wang and Tai Jen, Wen's parents, and T'an Fu (known as Ku Kung, the Old Duke), grandfather of Wen, who in 1326 B.C. left the principality of Pin after constant harassment by barbarous neighbors and was followed "along the western water courses / along their banks to the slopes of K'i," by hundreds of families who had lived under him and benefited by his virtue. It was here that the state of Chou was founded (Ode 237). In addition, we are taken back over a thousand years before Wen's time to the story of Chiang Yuan, a barren wife of the recently deceased King T'i Ku, who, having ceaselessly prayed for a child, during a sacrificial rite "poured wine / to the West sun" and "trod the Sky's spoor"—stepped in the footprint of God—was thereby impregnated, and subsequently gave birth to Hou Tsi, "J. Barleycorn," as Pound calls him, a god of agriculture at whose touch "broad beans . . . gave leaf suddenly" and "melons gat laughing brood" (Ode 245). The association of the Chou with the very image of fertility, who hands down the true Rite for the benefit of all generations, completes the total pattern of Chou virtue and establishes its identity with the forces of Heaven. The last figure in the gallery of ancestral archetypes is that of Duke Liu (Ode 250), who in 1796 B.C. moved his people to Pin, just as some 450 years later T'an Fu was to move them to Chou.

The recurrent theme of the pien odes (Odes 253–265) is simply that the Chou kings who ignore their birthright, the heritage of Wen, and thus flout the Ming of Heaven, are following the image of the Shang and are thereby courting destruction. The writer of the ya becomes the conscience of the past, the admonitory voice of heaven, who seeks to recall the errant king, in this case Li Wang (878–842 B.C.), to his proper destiny by appealing to him either directly or through his corrupt ministers. Actually these odes are not readily distinguishable from the pien "Hsiao Ya," for the crimes of Hsuan and Yu against nature and against the people seem really to be no less serious than those of Li Wang. Li wanted to accumulate all the money in the kingdom and to silence all complaints from the people as well as advice from his more sensitive ministers; after three years he was deposed and escaped into exile. A serious enough crime, but one that brought the dynasty no closer to ruin than that of Yu—and indeed Yu does reappear as the subject of the last ode of the "Ta Ya." The ta quality of the poems in this section, aside from their length, lies in their constant and explicit warning that Li has deliberately set his mind against heaven and that he has blindly cut himself off from his ancestry. That is perhaps one reason the T'ang decad, comprised wholly of odes of censure, opens with a poem in which Wen recites the crimes of the Shang, for this is the model of the Great Admonition, an explicit recollection of the central historical episode that may be implied in the "Hsiao Ya" but is never actually stated.

Set against the criticism of Li are the concluding odes of the "Ya," the praise of Hsuan in his early reign (Odes 258–263). As one might anticipate, such praise envisions Hsuan as carrying on the true traditions of Chou after the debacle of his father. A child upon the exile of Li, he came to the throne in 827 B.C., after a thirteen-year interregnum, to inherit a natural world still suffering from the disease inflicted on it by Li's evil feng: the drought that is the subject of the introductory ode in the sequence. The very fact that Hsuan prays to heaven and seeks to communicate with his ancestors, and that he wishes to assume full responsibility for the suffering ("would that it fell upon me, on my person only"), indicates his rectitude and at least the hope for salvation of the Chou. Hsuan's attempt to pacify and colonize the South (Odes 259–264), guided by the light of heaven and aided by loyal vassals, is the external expression of his virtue and the act by which the kingdom is preserved and the dynasty maintained. The tenor of the last two odes in the "Ta Ya," concerned with the corruption of Yu, is summarized in the concluding stanza of Ode 265:

> When the king (Süan) got the Decree here
> before you
> he had a Duke of Shao to uphold him
> who brought the state an hundred *li* in one
> day;
> Today they lose daily similar holding,
> and as to the nature of sorrow
> there are men who do not strive to grasp the
> antique.

Because of the quasi-didactic nature of these odes, a literary translation would necessarily depend almost solely upon a lyrical diction for its effect. Because they are plotless, the odes provide the translator with none of the usual epic attributes, the most important of which is the dramatic appeal in which some kind of empathy can be established. Although the mythical framework of the involvement of men and gods exists, its medium of expression is not so much narrative as revelatory.

As an introduction to Pound's treatment of this section, I should like to begin with some of the remarks of Hugh Kenner:

> Pound is able by drawing on dozens of chronological and formal conventions to convince us that we are handling, in English, an authentic Sacred Book with a long history. This is the *use* of his awesome technical mastery, of his ability to manage the

> most intricate effects with the air of improvising, or add an extra dimension to a small lyric by echoing as he renders its plain sense the mood of some vernacular genre or the turn of phrase of some familiar English anthology piece. The use of the Miracle Play idiom in portions of Part III is the most striking instance of this technique; the élan of the chronicler whose mind is on the most important facets of his subject comes through the rhythmic primitiveness of the "Creation" Odes as it would not through a more enameled surface.[4]

This is indeed a brilliant apology and in many ways justified, for in his handling of these odes Pound does in fact take full advantage of his lyrical talent. Here, for example, is the opening stanza of Ode 245 in which the birth of Hou Tsi is described:

> Mankind began when Kiang Yüan poured
> wine
> to the West sun and circling air
> and, against barrenness, trod the Sky's spoor.
> Then, as a sudden fragrance funnelled in
> and to its due place,
> a thunder-bolt took body there to be
> and dawn Hou Tsi, whom she bare on his day
> and suckled presently.

This stanza is everything that Kenner has ascribed to the odes in general, and it is true that throughout the section one will find more like it. But the matter does not rest here, for as soon as we begin the next stanza we find lines like, "Saith legend: was full moon, and effortless / the first birth was as a lamb's, no pain, no strain." One might say that this has an "air of improvisation," but if Pound had written "no sweat, no fret," the line could not have been much triter. A poem asserted in a detailed footnote to be a coronation ode and for nine stanzas translated as one, ends:

> The Lord's wagons be many,
> his fast horses trained better than any,

And a few verses will make a song
when there's a tune to drag it along.

(Ode 252)

It is not that a comparison between the verse and the king's horses is not in the original: "Our lord's chariots / Are many in number; / Our lord's horses, / well trained and swift. / So I have put together many verses / To make this song" (Waley). The trouble lies with the sing-song couplets and Pound's particular phraseology that represent anything but an "awesome technical mastery." Here are Pound's lines from an ode attributed to the Earl of Fan:

You smirk.
It's in the line of duty. Wipe off that smile, and
as our grandfathers used to say:
Ask the fellows who cut the hay. (Ode 254)

And here is Wen speaking:

King Wen said: So!
You brawl in the middle kingdom;
collect resentments and call it sincerity.
There is no light in your conscience
and your acts shed, therefore, no light
in your inwit, and you are left without
ministers,
without party.

. . . .

King Wen said: Huh . . .
Your noise is like bugs in the grass . . .

(Ode 255)

In one instance it is no duke, Chinese or otherwise, who is speaking; in the other, the prosaic rendering generates no emotion, genuine or false. Only with these serious reservations in mind can I agree with Kenner's assessment. Yet, as I have said, Kenner has his point. Consider, for example, the opening stanza of the first ode in the Wen decad (Ode 235) as rendered by Waley:

King Wên is on high;
Oh, he shines in Heaven!
Chou is an old people,
But its charge is new.
The land of Chou became illustrious,
Blessed by God's charge.
King Wên ascends and descends
On God's left hand, on His right.

But Pound, despite the obscurities of the etymological method, is able to reach epic elevation:

Bright, aloft, Wen, glitteringly,
Chou, tho' an old regime, gat new decree;
Had not Chou been there like the sun's fountainhead
the supernal seals had never caught sun's turn
that King Wen tread
up, down, to stand
with the heavenly veils to left hand and right hand.

Had Pound been consistent, the translations would have been one of the great literary documents of our times.

The sacrificial odes with which the Anthology concludes will appear to the reader of Pound as a more or less uniformly lyrical but highly repetitious and fairly obscure series of poems, a state of affairs differing only in degree from that confronting him in the preceding books. To the Confucian mind, however, the "Sung," representing as it does the ultimate discourse—that between man and ancestral spirit, present and past, living and dead—is the culmination of all the poetry that has preceded it. It is believed to have been placed last not because of its inferior importance, but because it signifies the fruition of Wen's influence: the era of peace and order during the reign of Ch'eng Wang, the third Chou king, who inherited the full benefits of the war of foundation recorded in the "Ya." As the final articulation of a rectified society that, through the person of the king, has bound itself to the past, the genre is itself a kind of logos or "verbal correlative" of a supreme moral condition of the mind and therefore an instrument par excellence for communication with heaven. Through prayers and "reports," the society at once announces and demonstrates its salvation.

The assigning of the greater part of the sacrificial odes contained in the Chou Sung, or first section, to the time of Ch'eng was clearly a logical necessity, although such a position has now become extremely controversial. All the odes of the "Sung" are "genuine" (cheng); thus they must proceed from a totally correct epoch, the last of which was that of Ch'eng Wang. Since the majority are directed to Wen and Wu, they could not have been written before Ch'eng's time. Whether one accepts this reasoning or not, one can at least appreciate the historical, philosophical, and moral impulses behind it: Ch'eng fulfills the semimythical history of the Chou by becoming the image of filial piety, devoting himself to the ancestral spirits of his father and grandfather, or, on a grand scale, to the ideals that earned the Ming of Heaven. In short, he brings to focus in his person a basic truth of Confucian ideology—that one's present glory is but a result of the achievements of one's ancestors.

One need hardly add that in the orthodox view the arrangement of the "Sung," like that of the preceding books, holds some kind of moral significance. As to the major divisions, the "Temple Odes of Chou" are believed to have appeared first for obvious reasons: they are the royal songs of the golden age. The second book, translated by Pound under the title "The Horse Odes of Lu," is, by honoring Hsi Kung, a reflection of the glory of his father, Chou Kung, the model of the virtuous advisor who preserved the throne for Ch'eng during his infancy by quelling the notorious Rebellion of the Brothers, and later organized the civil administration, an act that, by bringing order to the empire, allegedly made formalization of the "Sung" possible. The third book,

"The Odes of Shang," harkens back to that period of the previous dynasty that was a prototype, albeit inferior in achievement, to the great age of the Chou. All three subjects are worthy of being exalted in the "Sung" even though the last two, by their very nature, are eclipsed by the first.

The *Mao Shih Chu Shu* goes so far as to propose a moral purpose in the arrangement of the three decads of the "Temple Odes" as well, a moral purpose closely related to chronological development. Indeed, as we have seen repeatedly in the Chinese view of the kind of history expressed in the *Shih,* chronological development and the progress or retrogress of moral forces are synonymous. The "Ch'ing Miao" decad, the first, is asserted to have been created during the time of Ch'eng's accession at about age thirteen (1111 B.C.), with Chou Kung as his guardian. Ch'eng's virtue is in large part ascribed to Chou Kung, who educated him according to the principles established by Wen and Wu; yet even though the figure of the regent lies behind much of the "Sung," the glory must belong primarily to the king himself, for were he not of the "true race" the influence of his uncle would have been meaningless. In fact, in the first years of his reign, Ch'eng was blind to Chou Kung's virtues and, believing slander, allowed him to go into voluntary exile. Chou Kung's restoration was a triumph both of his own virtue and the natural qualities of his protégé.

The Confucian insistence that the first decad is associated with the early reign of Ch'eng is logical enough on a philosophical basis, although without much historical or textual justification. The feng of Wen Wang blows through the "Sung"; his son, as a youth, reflects his piety by singing praises of his father in the first decad. Similarly, because the son is filial, the reign is good, and the result is a bountiful harvest, reflected in the second decad, which is more or less associated with Ch'eng's manhood. Ostensibly, what occurs in the final decad is directly dependent on what occurred before it or somehow is associated with the later part of Ch'eng's reign.

I do not wish to foist this view of the "Sung" upon the reader, but if we are to speak of a Chinese paideuma we cannot but speak of it in these terms, if two millenia of Confucian commentary are to stand for anything in Chinese thought. On the other hand, Pound's conception of the paideuma in the "Sung" was, as in the other three sections, far from exact. I dare say that the mere idea of sacrificial odes being sung in the ideal society was sufficient in itself to satisfy him; as the apocalyptic translator, he fulfilled his mission when he transmitted to the reader an insight into the devotional mind of ancient China—the only moral import being that here was a society capable of undergoing a genuine religious experience.

Pound is, of course, justified in treating the "Sung" as a series of occasional pieces, but the matter doesn't end here, for the Western reader is being presented not with a number of songs for his historical or sociological edification, but with a series of consciously wrought odes that make no attempt to reflect the ultimately utilitarian purposes of their originals, and the entire impact of which depends upon their own literary merits. Read as such, without one's knowing anything about their actual background or meaning to the Confucian mind, the odes are extremely repetitious, a fact that may well be valued by Pound the moral educator and ignored by Pound the translator, but that is very much the problem of Pound the poet.

Consider, for instance, the entire first decad, the poems of which the reader of the translation will find almost indistinguishable from one another as far as content is concerned: the praise of Wen uttered in prayer and report. Yet, traditionally, each poem has its own particular character and function. Briefly: the first ode (266) is taken to be associated with the establishment of Ch'eng's new capital at Lo Yi in 1111 B.C.; the second is supposedly a report to the ancestors of the state of peace; the third is a song accompanying a military dance imitating a maneuver used by Wu during the great battle; the fourth is a song associated with the accession ceremony in 1155 B.C.; the fifth is a "celebration of ancient kings and dukes"; the sixth is a song honoring the heaven and earth; the seventh is a song honoring Wen in the newly established *Ming Tang* or "Hall of Light"; the eighth is a song honoring mountains during royal visits (made according to strict seasonal regulation, all movement by the king necessarily being in harmony with nature and the Will of Heaven); the ninth is a song honoring Wu; and the tenth is one honoring Hou Tsi. As might be expected, the orthodox scholar sees meaning in this particular arrangement. Wen is honored first for obvious reasons; because of Wen, Wu's victory over the Shang was possible, hence the military dance in Ode 268. Similarly, because of Wen, the princes are regulated and prove their devotion at Ch'eng's accession ceremony (Ode 269), and it is then possible for other ancestors to be honored (Ode 270). All other ceremonies follow in their proper order: the honoring of heaven and earth in the spring (Ode 271), the ceremony in the Ming Tang in autumn (Ode 272), the honoring of mountains and rivers during the royal expedition (Ode 273), the honoring of Wu for his own greatness, second to Wen (Ode 274), and finally the honoring of Hou Tsi—last, argues the *Mao Shu* curiously, because he is only a distant ancestor.

As for the odes of Lu, we find the subject to be Hsi Kung, son of Chou Kung, who was granted the lordship of Lu by Ch'eng. In referring to this section as the "Horse Odes," Pound is exaggerating, for in general Hsi is praised in the characteristic way, and the horse images appear only in the first and second odes. Legge has argued, with justice, that this section actually does not belong in the "Sung," since properly speaking the odes are neither royal nor sacrificial. "Confucius found them in Loo," he writes, "bearing the name of *Sung;* and it was not for him to do otherwise than simply edit them as he did." [5] In any event, the moral point of these odes is evident: Hsi Kung honors his ancestors, his virtuous ministers, and heaven, and thereby demonstrates the extensions of the feng of Wen Wang. A similar rationale is made for the appearance of the five Shang odes, which celebrate events that parallel those celebrated by the Chou. Here Ch'ing T'ang (T'ang), who founded the Shang dynasty (1766 B.C.), becomes the fountainhead of virtue and his wars against the previous dynasty (Hsia) become the central historical event (Odes 301, 302, 303). Also celebrated is Wu-ting, who ascended the throne in 1324 B.C. (Ode 305); Hsieh, the founder of the clan; Hsiang-t'u, his grandson; and I-yin, T'ang's loyal minister, corresponding to Chou Kung (Ode 304). The odes of Lu and Shang were supposedly included, then, not just because they existed, but because they were particularly relevant to the moral purposes of Kung.

The point here is not that one be convinced by this reasoning, especially in regard to the "Temple Odes," but merely that one appreciate that it is Chinese reasoning, and that whatever its distortions it is a culminating part of the vision of the *Shih* as an apocalyptic book. Unfortunately, if the entire Confucian view is rejected, what is left is merely of historical or sociological interest, and even these two interests are denied us in Pound's stylized and literary translation. The result is that we are faced with a series of odes that had meaning as occasional songs created for a specific purpose or as songs taken to be apocalyptic, but as creations in themselves, as English lyrics, they are, beyond a point, meaningless. The Western reader may respond to their aesthetic qualities, but he will quickly tire of their limited content.

What is interesting about this problem is that Pound's

metaphysic, far from being defeated by the nature of the material, actually thrives on it. That the theme of the "Sung" is unvarying is unimportant; what matters is the language in which it is expressed, a language that in itself is morally significant for no other reason than that it is "poetic," since in true poetry lies renovation. Pound was no doubt convinced that he was rendering the spirit of the original, recreating it in the only way that would be effective for the modern Western reader, but at this point one may well wonder whether the original had a transmittable spirit at all.

In practice, Pound's notions led, true enough, to the lyricizing of the "Sung," and this is the one section that is free of the "colloquial" idiom. The only danger inherent in the purely lyrical style is the occasional tendency to allow the requirements for an elevated tone to take precedence over the requirements for intelligibility. For example, here is a stanza from Ode 273:

> Solid and dexter order holdeth Chou
> at his light words to shake
> and none shake not,
> three fields (T'ien, Hao, and Wei)
> spirits awake . . .

Prosaically, but more clearly:

> Truly are the honour and succession come
> from it [heaven] to the House of Chow.
> To his movements
> All respond with tremulous awe.
> He has attracted and given rest to all spiritual
> Beings,
> Even to (the Spirits of) the Ho, and the
> highest hills. (Legge)

Pound's translation is based on a word-for-word reading that, as usual, avoids the abstract meaning inherent in the original and uses particles in their literal sense: 實 solid (and) 右 right, dexter 有 has 周 Chou, and so on. As is often the case, a word-by-word rendering of a foreign language turns out to be lyrical in English. In this instance, Pound sees the translation as being not only lyrical but closer to the realities of the Chinese language and therefore closer to the Chinese paideuma. In the original, however, common words are often used in obscure ways or to fill out the rhythm: 右 here refers to a position of honor; 序 means the succession, not order; 有 周 taken together means the House of Chou. The irony, of course, is that Pound is probably completely aware of the correct usage, which was before his eyes in the translations of Legge and Karlgren and laboriously explained in the footnotes of the former. He simply did not believe that correct usage was true usage, and we have the result before us: a lyrical reading that in this example slightly misses making sense. The "three fields" that Pound mentions are a quasi-etymological rendering of 疊 fear, or, as Legge puts it, "tremulous awe." 田 by itself means field, and, in the character, Pound has discovered three of them. Where the "T'ien, Hao, and Wei" come from, I have yet to learn.

As we have seen all along, Pound's pursuit of etymology takes him some distance from the original, but usually not out of sight. Throughout the "Ch'ing Miao" decad, for instance, there is a recurrence of light images, based not upon the Chinese abstraction but upon the elements in the characters or upon nothing at all. "Tensile is heaven's decree / in light . . . without end" (Ode 267) is pure innovation; "Light above heaven" (Ode 271) and "Light over sky" (Ode 273) are a rendering of 昊 , a particle carrying no meaning at all but composed of 日 sun, and 天 sky. In the same ode there appears "Light to the mind from Chou" from 明 bright, 昭 illustrious, and 有 周 the House of Chou. The reader may recognize here the same syntactical pattern as discussed above. In this instance Pound seeks his effect not through a word-by-word rendering but, again, through a quasi etymology in which he finds images particularly meaningful in his vision and yet still pertinent to the original.

Examples such as these might be cited indefinitely, but I think we have reached a point where we know fairly well what Pound's resources are as both translator and poet. In the past three chapters I have tried to show the means by which a mind, at once propagandistic and poetic, seeking orientation in a social literature yet wholly egocentric, bent on creating personae and experimenting in language yet really capable of speaking in only one voice, has tried to transform an ancient and alien document into a body of poetry meaningful to the present. The result has been a work at times painful in its whimsicality and bathos, yet often overwhelming in its lyrical power—characteristic of its author, in many ways characteristic of its age.

Notes

Chapter 1.

[1] Among those in a position to judge Pound's version, the Harvard Sinologue, Achilles Fang, and I. A. Richards, if his testimonial is any indication, have been enthusiastic. George Kennedy, of Yale, sees the work as having "loosed itself completely from any Chinese mooring" ("Fenollosa, Pound, and the Chinese character," *Yale Literary Magazine,* 126 (December, 1958), 36. Miss S. Y. Jung, in her unpublished doctoral dissertation, *Ezra Pound and China* (Seattle, University of Washington, 1955), includes a brief chapter on the Odes in which she calls them "new wine in old bottles." Hugh Kenner, in "Faces to the Wall," *Gnomon* (New York, McDowell and Obolensky, 1958), pp. 80–100, provides the best and most detailed critical commentary, but makes little reference to the originals.

[2] *Literary Essays* (London, Faber, 1954), p. 25. Two other elements of a poem are "melopoeia," music, and "phanopoeia," the "casting of images upon the visual imagination."

[3] Ode 16 as recorded in *The Classic Anthology Defined by Confucius* (Harvard University Press, Cambridge, 1954). All quotations of Pound's renderings are taken from this edition. The work was reprinted by New Directions in 1959 as *The Confucian Odes.*

[4] Of the modern school, foremost are Bernard Karlgren, Arthur Waley, G. Margoulies, and Marcel Granet. In the last century, James Legge, in his *Chinese Classics,* a heavily documented seven-volume translation, opposed the orthodox position expressed by the Han School, but generally accepted the more flexible and heterodox position of the famous Sung scholar, Chu Hsi. The major work on the continent at this time was that of S. Couvreur, who generally adhered to the Han School. Chinese opinion until the present century has been influenced by either the Han or the Sung interpretations, with the *Mao Shih Chu Shu* (a definitive critical collection of the most recent dynasty, the Ch'ing) inclining strongly to the former. The contemporary scholar, Hu Shih, was the first to repudiate publicly the entire Confucian position. Pound's sources were Legge, Karlgren, Couvreur, and the Latin translation of P. Lacharme (1752).

Chapter 2.

[1] Bk. III, Chap. VIII, 1; trans. James Legge in *The Four Books* (Shanghai, n.d.), p. 16.

[2] Waley makes the extremely interesting point that the remark "does not fit in with the original context" but that in "scriptural reinterpretation the fact . . . is of no consequence." *The Analects of Confucius,* Modern Library Edition (New York, Random House, n.d.), p. 95.

[3] Verse 4; in *The Four Books,* p. 2.

[4] *Li Chi* (*Book of Ceremonies*), chap. 17 ("Yueh Chi," "On Music"). The excerpt is taken from the translation of Lin Yu-tang in *The Wisdom of Confucius,* Modern Library Edition, p. 254.

[5] *Ibid.,* pp. 257–258.

[6] Trans. in Legge, *The Chinese Classics,* Vol. IV in two parts, *The She Ching or Book of Poetry* (Hong Kong, London Missionary Society, 1939), p. 37.* Vol. IV, 1, listed on binding as V; Vol. IV, 2, listed on binding as VI. Pages are numbered consecutively throughout both parts and are hereafter cited without volume numbers. Introductory pages have Roman numerals and have been marked with an asterisk by me to avoid confusion. The work will hereafter be cited as *She Ching;* except in this instance, I have adhered to the Wade-Giles system of romanization throughout the book.

[7] I have been presumptuous enough to take some liberties with Legge's translation, which I feel is misleading. He renders "The feelings move inwardly" but the preposition in this case seems ambiguous and the context calls for the feelings to move "from within." See *She Ching,* p. 34.*

[8] *She Ching,* pp. 35–36.*

[9] "Rectification of terms." Usually miswritten in Pound as "*ching ming.*"

[10] *She Ching,* p. 50.*

[11] *Ibid.,* p. 36.*

[12] *Analects,* Bk. XVII, 9; in *The Four Books,* pp. 156–157.

[13] *She Ching,* p. 34.*

[14] *Ibid.,* p. 46.

[15] *Ibid.,* p. 55.

[16] *Ibid.,* p. 349.

[17] *Ibid.,* p. 67.

[18] *Ibid.,* p. 43.*

[19] *Ibid.,* p. 35.

[20] *Ibid.,* pp. 303–304.

Chapter 3.

[1] *Guide to Kulchur* (New York, n.d.), pp. 255 and 283. Notice also Pound's remarks in *ABC of Reading:* "Music begins to atrophy when it departs too far from the dance . . . poetry begins to atrophy when it gets too far from music." (New York, New Directions, 1960), p. 14.

Pound's conception of music and its relation to poetry goes back to his imagist period.

[2] (New York, 1935), p. 21.

[3] *Ibid.*, p. 15.

[4] Pound's introduction to his translation of the *Analects* (London, Peter Owen, 1956), p. 8.

[5] *Guide to Kulchur*, pp. 28 and 121.

[6] Reprinted in Pound's *Instigations* (New York, Boni and Liveright, 1920), pp. 382–383.

[7] *Ibid.*, p. 364.

[8] George Kennedy, *op. cit.*, has a detailed attack on Fenollosa's ideas in general.

[9] Actually, there are four more categories of characters. Besides imitative symbols and phonetic compounds, L. Weiger in *Chinese Characters* (Ho Chien Fu, Catholic Mission Press, 1915) lists indicative symbols, logical combinations, ideographs with extended meanings, and false borrowings. See Vol. I, pp. 6 ff.

[10] I am indebted to Professor Harold Shadick of Cornell University for this translation.

[11] See Waley's *Book of Songs* (New York, Grove Press, 1960), p. 33. Although Waley has rearranged the odes topically and therefore has used a nonstandard numbering system, a table of correlation with the standard system appears in the appendix. All quotations from Waley are from this edition and no further reference will be made to it.

[12] Clark Emery in *Ideas into Action* (Coral Gables, University of Miami Press, 1958), *passim.*

[13] Variant readings exist, however, as Legge points out, with another school maintaining that the ode is reproaching licentiousness. I have given the reading more widely accepted by the orthodox scholars.

[14] Notice the reasoning in the *Analects:* "I hate those who with their sharp mouths overthrow kingdoms and families" (XVII, 17).

Chapter 4.

[1] *Festivals and Songs of Ancient China,* trans. E. D. Edwards (New York, Dutton, 1932), p. 85.

[2] *She Ching*, pp. 30–31.

[3] This ode has been variously interpreted. Although in Pound's version one would hardly recognize the logic, the Preface, as Legge records it, asserts that "appearances were against the lady; but to herself she was justified in her course. People would infer from seeing the hole made by a sparrow that it was provided with a horn, though in reality it has none," and so forth (*She Ching*, p. 27). In other words, the images here refer to the lady instead of to the lover, as they seem to in Pound's version. This kind of ambiguity is characteristic.

[4] Karlgren calls this ode a song in honor of a girl who is going to be married. "First the girls of the region are praised as desirable but not easily attained; then this girl, who is setting out on her marriage jour-

ney, is eagerly served by her comrades, who feed the horses for her." *Book of Odes* (Stockholm, Museum of Far Eastern Antiquities, 1950), p. 6.

[5] Waley, p. 60.

[6] Thus Legge states in regard to a similar ode: "How did Confucius give such a vile piece a place in the *She*? and how is its existence reconcilable with his statement that all the odes might be summed up in one sentence—'Have not a single depraved thought'? It is replied that the sage introduced this ode, showing, without blaming, the evil of the time . . . not afraid to leave his readers to form their own opinion about them" (*She Ching*, p. 80).

[7] *Op. cit.*, pp. 214–215.

[8] I might add at this point that Pound's epigraphs and notes are usually no more than external devices used to suggest Western equivalents. He is occasionally pedantic, as in the note to Ode 281, and sometimes whimsical, as in the note to Ode 246.

[9] *Gnomon*, p. 98.

CHAPTER 5.

[1] See *Analects*, XVI, 2.

[2] See also Ode 206.

[3] The *vitex negundo* is a North American, not a Chinese, tree, incidentally.

[4] Granet, for example, says the ode refers to a betrothal. Pound's "would I could share that shrub's unconsciousness," an "orthodox" reading, is translated by Granet as "What joy that thou hast no *acquaintance!*" and correspondingly in the other stanzas, "What joy thou hast no husband," "What joy thou hast no wife!" This argument depends on the ambiguity of the Chinese word "*chih*," which, Granet asserts, means "mate" as well as "knowledge."

[5] "Construction" odes appear in number throughout the ya. One of the chief signs of a king's glory, especially moral, is his foundation of a capital. Granet points out in *Chinese Civilization* that a chief epic prototype is the divine or semidivine figure conquering the wilderness. As both Legge and Pound tell us, the Ting star signifies the end of field work and the time for construction. In the historical reading, the subject is Wen Kung, a duke of Yung, who, adhering to the rites, refuses to begin construction until the proper time is signalled in the heavens.

[6] Possibly ironic.

[7] *Instigations*, p. 17.

CHAPTER 6.

[1] See *Gnomon*, p. 88.

[2] I have used one of Pound's sources here: Père Joseph de Mailla's *Histoire Generale de la Chine* (Paris, P. D. Pierres, 1777). The quotation is from Vol. I, p. 238. For the reader interested in more recent studies of this period, I recommend Friedrich Hirth's *The Ancient*

History of China (New York, Columbia University Press, 1911), H. G. Creel's *The Birth of China* (New York, Reynall and Hitchcock, 1937), Henry Maspero's *La Chine Antique* (Paris, Impr. Nationale, 1955), and Marcel Granet's *Chinese Civilization* (New York, Meridian, 1959).

[3] *The Religion of China* (Glencoe, Ill., Free Press, 1951), p. 113.

[4] *Gnomon*, p. 90.

[5] *She Ching*, p. 611.